NOTE.– 1. The tonnage of the engine room spaces below the upper deck is .... tons, and the tonnage of the total spaces framed in above the upper deck for propelling machinery and for light and air is 98·71 tons.

NOTE.– 2. The undermentioned spaces above the upper deck are not included in the cubical contents forming the ship's register tonnage:

Forecastle L. 39'0 = 61.17 Tons

NOTE.– 3. The location and tonnage of the boatswain's store rooms are as follows:–

Below Deck Forward = 44·29 Tons.

Name of Master	Certificate of Service/Competency No.

Names, residence, and description of the owners, and number of sixty-fourth shares held by each owner.

15th June 1962. Maxport Steamship Company Ltd., having its principal place of business at, 104 Dock Street, Newport, in the County of Monmouth. Thirty

C 345A

F 2328 (July 1979)

THE "USK" SHIPS

THE "USK" SHIPS

History of a Newport Shipping Venture

BY

P. M. HEATON

THE STARLING PRESS LTD
Printers & Publishers
Risca Newport Gwent
Great Britain
1982

ISBN 0 9507714 1 4

Published by P. M. Heaton, Pontypool, Gwent NP4 0QF

Printed by the Starling Press Ltd., Risca, Newport Gwent NP1 6YB

AUTHOR

Paul Michael Heaton was born at New Inn, Pontypool in 1944 and was educated at Greenlawn Junior School in New Inn and the Wern Secondary School at Sebastopol. At fifteen he left school and commenced employment, at first in a local store and then with a builders' merchant. A year later he was appointed as a Deck Cadet in the Merchant Navy, with the Lamport and Holt Line of Liverpool, and served in their vessels *Chatham, Constable* and *Romney* usually in the Brazil and River Plate trades. He joined the Monmouthshire Constabulary (now Gwent) in 1963 and has served at Abergavenny, Cwmbran, Newport, the Traffic Department (Motor Cycle Section) and as the Force Public Relations Officer at Police Headquarters, Croesyceiliog. He now holds the rank of Inspector.

He has always maintained an interest in maritime history, and since 1977 has had numerous articles published in the magazine *Sea Breezes*. He specialises in the history of South Wales shipping companies, and has had three previous books published—*Reardon Smith 1905-1980, The Redbrook: A Deep-Sea Tramp* and with H. S. Appleyard—*The Baron Glanely of St. Fagan's and W. J. Tatem Ltd.*

ACKNOWLEDGEMENTS

I would like to thank all those who have helped in the compilation of this volume, particularly:—

Mr. Paul Treverton Jones, Llantarnam.

Mr. Brian Ford Treverton Jones, Newport.

Mrs. Sara Rainforth, Raglan.

Mr. E. N. Taylor, Gosport.

Mr. David Burrell, Sevenoaks.

Mr. A. Duncan, Gravesend.

Mr. R. Wiltshire, Pontypool.

Mr. L. Coombes, Pontypool.

Mr. A. Hearn, Newport.

Messrs, G. H. Somner, H. S. Appleyard, K. O'Donoghue, P. L. White, the late Mr. L. Gray and the late Rev. D. Ridley Chesterton of the World Ship Society Central Record Team.

British Transport Docks Board, Newport.

The National Maritime Museum, London.

Skyfotos Ltd., New Romney, Kent.

World Ship Photo Library.

The Registrar of Shipping, Newport.

Gwent County Archivist, Croesyceiliog.

Cardiff Central, Newport and Cwmbran Reference Libraries.

Ailsa Shipbuilding Co. Ltd., Troon.

Austin and Pickersgill Ltd., Sunderland.

Mr. J. Lingwood, Sunderland.

Mr. C. J. M. Carter, the Editor of "Sea Breezes" for his continued advice.

And lastly to my wife and family for their patience and support throughout.

CONTENTS

Author 5
Acknowledgements 6
List of Illustrations 8
1. Introduction 11
2. The Development of the Port of Newport Before 1880... 13
3. The Origins of the Jones Family and the Formation of Richard W. Jones and Company 15
4. The Entry into Shipowning 17
5. Expansion of Shipowning Interests 21
6. Voyage Details of S.S. "Alassio" 1.1.1889-15.7.1889 ... 25
7. The Death of Richard William Jones and Resulting Reorganisation 35
8. Voyage Details of S.S. "Alassio" 18.7.1898-3.7.1899 ... 38
9. The Death of Thomas Jones. Control of the Business Passes to Bonn Henry Jones 42
10. Formation of the Uskside Steamship Co. Ltd. 44
11. Entry Into the Esparto Trade and the Subsequent Expansion 46
12. The Depression 50
13. The Second World War 53
14. The Post-War Recovery 55
15. A New Ship is Ordered 60
16. The Last Ten Years 67
17. Appendix One—Partners in Richard W. Jones and Company 73
18. Appendix Two—Fleet List 74
19. Appendix Three—Ships Managed on Behalf of the Ministry of War Transport 80
20. Appendix Four—S.S. "Camargo"—Share Transactions 1880-1893 82
21. Appendix Five—S.S. "Uskbridge"—Transcript of Ship's Register 88

LIST OF ILLUSTRATIONS

1. Delivered to Richard W. Jones and Company in 1883 the "Alassio" had been built by the Strand Slipway Company, Sunderland. The ship is shown aground in the Humber. (*K. O'Donoghue*).
2. The "Elorrio" joined the fleet in 1894 from the Sunderland yard of Wm. Pickersgill and Sons. (*York Collection*).
3. The first "Uskmouth" was built in 1916 by J. Priestman and Company, Sunderland. (*National Maritime Museum*).
4. Acquired in 1921 from other owners the "Uskside" (2) had been built four years earlier by Craig, Taylor and Co. Ltd., Stockton. (*A. Duncan*).
5. The "Uskside" (2) remained in the fleet until 1931. (*York Collection*).
6. One of seven steamers built for the firm by the Burntisland Shipbuilding Co. Ltd., the "Uskbridge" (1) was delivered in 1924. (*World Ship Photo Library*).
7. The first "Uskbridge" heavily laden with esparto grass. (*A. Duncan*).
8. The first "Uskport" entered the fleet of the Uskport Steamship Co. Ltd. in 1925. (*York Collection*).
9. The steamer "Uskport" of 1925. (*A. Duncan*).
10. (Also Front Cover). A striking view of the "Uskmouth" (2) which was delivered to the Uskside Steamship Co. Ltd. in 1928. (*National Maritime Museum*).
11. The "Uskvalley" of 1929. (*National Maritime Museum*).
12. Launch Party for the "Uskside" (3) at Burntisland on November 26 1936. The ship was launched by Mrs. Sara Rainforth.
13. The "Uskside" (3) enters the water at Burntisland on November 26, 1936.
14. Launch Party at Burntisland for the "Uskbridge" of 1940. From the Left: Guy Treverton Jones, Lady Ayre, Mrs. Joyce Treverton Jones (who launched the ship), and Sir Amos Ayre.
15. Built in 1944 as the "Empire Osborne" the second "Uskport" joined the fleet in 1946. (*Skyfotos Ltd.*).
16. The "Uskport" in the English Channel on passage from North Africa to the Firth of Forth with a cargo of esparto grass. (*Skyfotos Ltd.*).
17. The fourth "Uskside" was laid down as the "Empire Warner" for the Ministry of War Transport, but completed for the Uskside Steamship Co. Ltd. in 1946. (*A. Duncan*).
18. In the English Channel, the "Uskside" was on passage from the St. Lawrence to the Thames with a cargo of pulp wood. (*Skyfotos Ltd.*).
19. The "Uskside" outward bound with a cargo of coal from the North East Coast to Italy. (*Skyfotos Ltd.*).
20. The "Uskmouth" (3) was acquired in 1951. She is shown homeward bound with a cargo of esparto grass. (*Skyfotos Ltd.*).
21. The third "Uskmouth" in ballast. (*World Ship Photo Library*).

22. Launch of the "Uskbridge" (3) at Troon on February 24, 1959 by Mrs. Sara Rainforth.

23. The "Uskbridge" as built by the Ailsa Shipbuilding Co. Ltd., Troon. (*A. Duncan*).

24. "Uskbridge" (3). (*World Ship Photo Library*).

25. Lengthening of the "Uskbridge" at Troon: Entering dry dock at 11am on May 1, 1962.

26. Lengthening of the "Uskbridge" at Troon: Winch and wires set up to pull bow half forward at 2.30pm on May 10, 1962.

27. Lengthening of the "Uskbridge" at Troon: The pull completed at 4pm on May 10, 1962 leaving a forty foot gap.

28. Lengthening of the "Uskbridge" at Troon: Now out of dry dock, on June 26, 1962. The ship sailed the following day.

29. The lengthened "Uskbridge" (3) in the English Channel. (*Skyfotos Ltd.*).

30. The third "Uskport" was acquired in 1962 from the Tate and Lyle Group. (*A. Duncan*).

31. The "Uskport" was the only motorship to enter the fleet. (*Skyfotos Ltd.*).

32. The Offices of Richard W. Jones and Company 1929-1968, at 104 Dock Street, Newport.

1. INTRODUCTION

During my numerous visits to Barry Docks during the 1950s, and having been brought up in Monmouthshire, I was fascinated to see the Newport registered steamships *Uskport, Uskside* and *Uskmouth* on their periodic visits to the port for attention at the shiprepairing facility of C. H. Bailey Ltd. These three war-built ships represented the whole fleet of Richard W. Jones and Company, a family shipowning business and were registered in the ownership of the Uskport Steamship Co Ltd. or the Uskside Steamship Co. Ltd. I was left with an impression of three ships which were obviously maintained to quite high standards and always appeared to be clean and well turned out. This view was shared by others; in his book *Merchant Ships of the World 1910-1929* Laurence Dunn commented:—

> Although primarily engaged in the coal trade, the *Usk* ships were quite outstanding for their smart appearance, having white-painted islands, superstructure and masts, when the use of dirt-concealing brown was very common for such vessels.

In 1961 I was at Dublin when I saw the *Uskside* again discharging phosphate on behalf of Messrs. Gouldings Fertilisers and being the first occasion that I saw an "Usk" ship on its business of carrying cargo, I was impressed by the sheer workmanlike appearance of the ship and the noise of her steam winches hammering away further enforced the view.

Having taken an interest in maritime history, and as Richard W. Jones and Company were at that time one of the few surviving South Wales shipowners operating in the intermediate tramp trades, I decided to undertake some research. In consequence I visited the firm's offices at 104 Dock Street, Newport, where I met one of the partners, Mr. Brian Ford Treverton Jones, who gave me invaluable assistance with my project. Unfortunately in 1968 the business closed and I put the results of my research to one side. In 1977 I was fortunate enough to contact Mr. Paul Treverton Jones, the brother of Brian, who further helped me and as a result I compiled a history of the firm which appeared in the shipping magazine *Sea Breezes* in February, 1978.

However, in recent years I have researched the histories of a number of South Wales shipowning ventures and have been amazed to learn how few of these were founded by native born Welshmen. The majority were formed by men from North Devon, Cornwall and Jersey, who were originally shipping clerks, seafarers or merchants. They had moved to the area and set up businesses coincidental with the development of the South Wales ports resulting from the expansion of the coal fields and iron-works of the hinterland brought about by the improvement in communications. Thus my fascination with the partnership of Richard W. Jones and Company is in part due to the fact that it was founded by a family which had its origins in South Wales, or more particularly

Monmouthshire itself. As a result I decided to compile this expanded volume devoted to the firm's history and readers should glean from it the obvious enterprise that the founders and subsequent generations have shown.

I have started with details of the development of the port of Newport before 1880, followed by the origins of the Jones family, the formation of the business and the various developments until its subsequent closure in 1968. I have endeavoured to give as comprehensive an account as possible of the trades served by their ships, but in this connection should point out that specific records of the venture do not exist. Also included are details of crew members taken from a sample of Agreements and Accounts of Crews which I was able to inspect at the Gwent County Archives Office.

I hope that readers will be left with an honest impression of what was involved in the operation of a small family shipowning venture over a period of almost a century and how it developed from their initial principle activity as merchants trading in coal, iron ore and pitwood.

P. M. HEATON

October, 1982

2. THE DEVELOPMENT OF THE PORT OF NEWPORT BEFORE 1880

The establishment in 1875 of the partnership of Richard W. Jones and Company was a reflection of the growth of Newport as an important industrial centre and major sea port. An account of this venture would not be complete without a review of this development and the following is a passage from the British Transport Docks Board's Historical Notes on Newport Docks.

> Although there is evidence that its history goes back to very ancient times, Newport is a comparatively young town, for it was not until the early part of the 19th Century that its development as an important industrial centre and sea port really commenced. The first stage was the completion of the Monmouthshire Canal and Sirhowy Tram-road. These two undertakings opened up access to the rich coalfields of the Eastern and Western Valleys of Monmouthshire, and greatly facilitated the conveyance of coal to Newport for shipment from the jetties and wharves located along the banks of the River Usk. By 1830, the berthage accommodation in the river was proving inadequate to meet the requirements of a rapidly expanding export trade, and the urgent need for additional facilities provided the motive for the formation of the Newport Dock Company. In 1835, the Company obtained parliamentary powers for the construction of the first enclosed dock which was 1.62 hectares in extent and opened in 1842, but the increasing demands of shipping continued swiftly to outpace the facilities offering, and before long, even the new dock was heavily congested with vessels seeking a loading berth. Further parliamentary powers were obtained, and in 1858 a 3.04 hectare extension was opened; the new dock then became known as the Town Dock. In the meantime, railway development in Monmouthshire and South Wales had proceeded apace, in line with the expansion of the coalfields and the construction and development of iron works. The improved transport facilities and increasing overseas demand for high quality coals underlined the need for still further dock accommodation at Newport and in July, 1865 the Alexandra (Newport) Dock Act received royal assent. This Act authorised the forming of the Alexandra (Newport) Dock Company and the promoters were empowered to construct a new dock, 11.74 hectares in extent, entirely separate from and closer to the mouth of the river than the Town Dock. The new Alexandra Dock (which later became known as the Alexandra North Dock) was opened in 1875, and at that time marked a considerable advance in the dock accommodation of the port.

Another indication of the growth of Newport was the town's population which in 1800 was just over 1,000; fifty years later it had risen to 20,000 and by 1900 was 67,000.

Coal shipments from Newport in 1797 (the year after the completion of the Monmouthshire Canal) had amounted to 6,939 tons, but in 1875, the year that the new dock opened, the shipments including coal shipped coastwise and bunker coal, had risen to 983,474 tons. However, in the five years following this they had more than doubled to 2,072,240 tons. Newport became the major iron ore importing port in South Wales, with iron ore imports in 1875 through the new Alexandra North Dock alone amounting to 18,728 tons, but rising in the next five years to the staggering figure of 481,249 tons.

3. THE ORIGINS OF THE JONES FAMILY AND THE FORMATION OF RICHARD W. JONES AND COMPANY

The origins of the Jones family can be traced to Pontypool in the Eastern Valley of Monmouthshire, where considerable development had taken place in connection with iron works prior to the 19th Century. The father of the founders of Richard W. Jones and Company was one Thomas Jones who was the agent to the Ebbw Vale Iron and Steel Company, a business which owned iron foundries and collieries at Ebbw Vale, iron ore mines at Northampton and in Spain, to mention a part of their interests. Thomas who had moved to Newport, operated from his home at 23 Stow Hill, and was responsible for the company's commercial activities outside Ebbw Vale.

Thomas had married Anne Eliza Pearse of Bristol and they had a family of six children, Richard William, born in 1843; Thomas born in 1844; Alfred, who died in infancy; Margaret; Alfred Wilkinson and John Henry who was born in 1853 but was better known as Bonn. As was usual in those days, they were a close family and Richard with the support and influence of his father, in 1864 became established as the agent to the Pontypool Iron Company at the comparatively early age of twenty-one. Like his father he built up extensive connections both in the United Kingdom and abroad and in consequence in 1872 entered into business on his own account as a metal broker at 70 Dock Street, Newport. In this capacity he purchased iron ore and other materials on behalf of a number of industrial concerns in South Wales, but principally for those in Monmouthshire.

During 1875, coinciding with a considerable expansion of trade through Newport brought about by the opening of the new Alexandra North Dock, Richard was joined in partnership by his brother Thomas and thereafter they traded as Richard W. Jones and Company. By this time the business was expanding and they had become merchants trading in coal, iron ore and pitwood. In this connection they purchased coal in South Wales and arranged its sale at home and overseas, which involved close liaison with coal importers particularly in Spain and Italy. The iron ore was purchased on behalf of iron works not only in Monmouthshire but throughout South Wales, the Midlands and the North East. Thirdly, they bought pitwood for use in collieries, principally in Monmouthshire and as with the coal and iron ore, arranged shipment, initially through the offices of a third party.

The two brothers quickly became established and were leading members of the local community. Richard, who had a full face beard, married Helen Mullock of the well-known Newport family who were in business as stationers, a venture that has survived to the present day.

He was a Justice of the Peace and lived originally at Cross House, Stow Hill, later at Brighton Villas, Woodland Road, and finally at "Caer Gwyn", Caerau Park. He had five children, none of whom entered the business.

Thomas junior also lived in fashionable areas of the town, at 23 Bridge Street, and later 2 Clytha Square. He was, like his brother, a worthy citizen and a Justice of the Peace; he served on the local council, became an Alderman and was the Mayor of Newport in 1892. He is however, best remembered for his association with Allt-yr-yn Hospital. In 1892, with Theophilus Beynon (another shipowner), Doctor, later Sir Abraham Garrod Thomas and others, he founded the Newport based evening newspaper *The South Wales Argus* which has been published continuously ever since, a connection which has lasted through other members of the family for ninety years. He married Annie Jane Wilson Duffield and they had one daughter, who remained a spinster. The Jones family were of Liberal persuasion and attended the Victoria Road Congregational Church.

4. THE ENTRY INTO SHIPOWNING

Having been in partnership for a little over four years, their venture as merchants was proving so successful that Richard and Thomas decided to expand their interests and saw that there were great opportunities in shipowning. Much of their business involved arranging for the charter through third parties of ships to carry the cargoes, particularly of coal, which they were despatching overseas. In the latter part of 1879 they decided to enter shipowning on their own account and signed a contract with Wm. Pickersgill and Sons of Sunderland for the construction of a steamship designed for the intermediate trades. This ship, of the raised quarter deck type, was completed in July, 1880 as Pickersgill's yard number 47, it was of 948 gross tons and was given the Italian name of *Camargo*.

On July 27, the vessel was registered at the Custom House at Newport—entry number 5 in 1880 and was allocated the Official Number 79170. Thomas, who was to be responsible for the day to day management of the ship and additional vessels acquired later, was registered as the Managing Owner, whilst Richard was entered as the joint registered owner. Ships are registered as being divided into 64 shares and it was the custom to raise part of the capital for such a venture by selling some of these to those wishing to participate, most of whom were people associated with the partners in business, or friends and relatives. This was to be the case with the new ship and within five weeks of taking delivery of the *Camargo* 21 shares were transferred by the partners as follows:—

Date	*Shareholder*	*No. of Shares*
27.7.1880	Thomas Kemp, Master Mariner, 4 Eveswell Terrace, Maindee, Newport	1
27.7.1880	John Henry Robinson, Railway Contractor, Westminster Chambers, Westminster	2
27.7.1880	Thomas Reynolds, Civil Engineer, 3 Clements Lane, London	2
28.7.1880	George Louis Morton, Engineer, Farlton Court, Harlesdon, Road, Willesden, Middlesex	2
30.7.1880	Henry Tothill, Analytical Chemist, 5 Park Street, Newport	2
30.7.1880	William Mullock, Stationer, Newport	1
30.7.1880	Michael Thomas Brian, Coal Shipper, 1 Clytha Crescent, Newport	3

Date	Shareholder	No. of Shares
31.7.1880	Rowland John Nicholas, Shipping Agent, 72 Stow Hill, Newport James Henderson Winn, Shipping Agent, York Place, Newport Jointly	1
31.7.1880	Edward Handfield Morton, Engineer, 12 Eaton Road, Llaughton, Birkenhead, Chester	2
6.8.1880	James Stratton, Farmer, Chilcombe, Winchester, Hampshire	4
31.8.1880	William Denton, Ship Surveyor, Kymin Terrace, Penarth, Glamorgan	1

This left the partners with the balance of 43 shares, but many of these were sold during the next year as their reputation as shipowners became more widely known, therefore spreading the risk somewhat. The net earnings of the ship were divided into 64 parts and subsequently distributed to the shareholders. Before this was achieved, a fee which would have been between 2% to 3% of the gross earnings of the vessel was taken by the partnership as a management fee and was in return for having to maintain offices and staff and arranging the charters etc. This sum would have been another means by which the partners would have increased their capital. Of the above shareholders William Mullock was Richard's father-in-law, William Denton was the person responsible for working out the ship's specification with the shipbuilders on behalf of Richard W. Jones and Company, and was their marine superintendent. Others were closely associated with the partners, but many did not have any connection and I must assume that they relished what they saw as a good opportunity to invest in a profitable venture. A full list of the share transactions in relation to the *Camargo* for the thirteen years that she was in Richard W. Jones and Company's fleet is produced as Appendix 4 to this volume.

The partners appointed Captain Thomas Le Pelley of Brock Cottage, St. Sampsons, Guernsey, as their first Master. On January 7, 1881 they allowed him to take one share in the *Camargo*. This was a wise move much practised at that time as it ensured that the person in charge of the vessel while it was out of sight of the owners was committed by his interest to take all possible steps to maintain the profitability of the ship, for he had much to gain himself. A result of this would see the vessel running as smoothly and economically as possible and undue delays in port kept to a minimum.

The ship was placed in the trades, generally with coal outwards from Newport, but occasionally from other South Wales ports or Hull. This was destined for the coaling station at Gibraltar or Spanish and

Italian ports. The usual homeward cargo was iron ore from Huelva on the Atlantic coast of Spain to Garston on the Mersey. Occasionally the ship went to Hull or South Wales ports with ore or carried grain from Italy to London. The advantage of taking coal outwards to Gibraltar and iron ore homewards from Huelva was that these ports are very close, and thereby reduced to a minimum the ballast passage, that part of the voyage when the vessel was not earning any income.

These trades were carried on by a number of South Wales owners, but the normal routine was in fact out to Italy with coal and homewards to Europe with grain from the Black Sea and later, particularly with the Cardiff owners who generally operated larger vessels, coal outwards to Brazil and the River Plate and homewards with grain from the latter region. Major interests in the trades to Spain were exercised by the Cardiff owners John Cory and Sons and Morel Brothers and Company, who owned mines in the Bilbao region and who had to an extent taken control of iron ore imports to the United Kingdom. On occasions the Jones' ships carried homeward iron ore cargoes on behalf of one or other of these firms.

During January, 1881 the partners' brother Alfred Wilkinson Jones took one share in the *Camargo*. Alfred who lived at Dash Wood House, London, was a mechanical engineer and never became engaged in the business, preferring to carry out his own occupation, but nevertheless actively supporting his older brothers in theirs. So pleased were the partners with the new venture and so successful was the *Camargo* operating, that in the Summer of 1881 they placed an order with Osborne, Graham and Company, Sunderland, for the construction of a larger vessel of a basically similar design. This steamer was completed in March, 1882 as the *Salerno,* named to reflect their trading interests. This selection of Italian names for their ships was to be carried on by the partners for over thirty years. The *Salerno* was registered at the Custom House, Newport on March 20, 1882, and exactly a week later they transferred 19 shares as follows:—

Shareholders	*No. of Shares*
Anne Eliza Jones, Widow, of 1 Clytha Square, Newport	5
Alfred Wilkinson Jones, Inspecting Engineer, of Dashwood House, New Broad Street, London	2
William Denton, Naval Architect and Ship Broker, of Penarth	1
Thomas Le Pelley, Master Mariner, of Newport	1
Rowland John Nicholas, Shipping Agent, of 72 Stow Hill, Newport	1
Thomas Lane, Shipwright, of 24 Raglan Street, Newport	1
Henry Ernest Baddeley, Commercial Clerk, of 11 Herbert Street, Newport	1
Michael Brian, Coal Shipping Contractor, of 26 Lime Street, Newport	2

Shareholders	*No. of Shares*
Michael Thomas Brian, Coal Shipping Contractor, of 26 Bridge Street, Newport	2
Thomas Limbery, Surgeon, of Newport	1
James Willcox Alsop, Solicitor, of 12 Castle Street, Liverpool	2

Anne Eliza Jones, who took five shares, was the partners' mother. After their father had died the previous year, she had moved from Stow Hill to 1 Clytha Square, next door to Thomas, further illustrating the closeness of the family. Her support for her sons was boundless as will be shown in some of the later transactions relating to their other vessels. Brother Alfred now had two shares in this ship together with his one in the *Camargo*. Many of the other shareholders were connected to the partners through business interests and some ensured a double interest; hence the shipwright with a share in the vessel who could be expected to obtain the work on it during its calls at the port. Captain Le Pelley was appointed to command the new ship and took one share, his interest in the *Camargo* being transferred back to the partners. By this time he had moved his home from the Channel Islands to Newport.

After appointing Captain Le Pelley to the command of the *Salerno,* they obtained the services of Captain Walter Runciman of 12 Salmon Street, South Shields to take over the *Camargo*. Three months later one share was transferred to this new Master.

Having owned the *Salerno* for seven months, the partners were approached by Scrutton, Sons and Company of London with an offer to buy the ship. At this time trade for shipowners was particularly good and Scrutton's who were anxious to take advantage of this could not wait to build a new vessel and made an exceptionally good offer for the ship. The partners decided to take advantage of this, and in doing so, not only yielded a handsome profit to themselves, but also to the other holders of 64th shares in the vessel. These must have been pleased, as many of them invested in one or more of the steamers which were subsequently delivered to Richard W. Jones and Company.

A further reflection on the sale of the *Salerno* indicates that Richard and Thomas considered themselves to be merchants first and shipowners second. Being merchants it was their primary function to make money by buying commodities, coal, ore and timber at a given price and disposing of same at a profit. The sale of the *Salerno* would, to them, have been a transaction made on the same principle. They were obviously sound business men.

The *Salerno* had a long career, remaining under the British flag until 1897. Having passed through various owners, Swedish and Norwegian, she was lost on May 2, 1918 when she was wrecked off the Cornish Coast near Godrevy Lighthouse while on passage from Swansea to Rouen with a cargo of coal.

5, EXPANSION OF SHIPOWNING INTERESTS

The sale of the *Salerno* increased their available capital and the operation of their steamer *Camargo,* having convinced them of the viability of shipowning as a complimentary activity to their main venture as merchants, Richard and Thomas set about expanding their interests in shipowning. In a most ambitious project in the months following the sale of the *Salerno* they signed contracts for the construction of three steamships each of around 1,200 gross tons with shipbuilders at Sunderland. All three contracts were signed with different yards in order to obtain as early as possible delivery of the ships. The first vessel, the *Alassio* was completed by the Strand Slipway Company in November, 1883, followed by the *Bergamo* from Wm. Pickersgill and Sons in February, 1884, and finally the *Durango* from Osbourne Graham and Company later in the year.

The partners were now operating a fine fleet of four ships. However, while a large number of 64th shares were taken by relatives, friends and others, the building of these three ships within a period of less than a year stretched their financial resources to the limit. As a result the partners mortgaged their interests in the ships as follows:—

Having taken delivery of the *Bergamo* from Wm. Pickersgill and Sons during February, 1884 the partners mortgaged 33 shares (*Bergamo* Mortgage "A") to William and Christopher Pickersgill jointly on July 26, 1884, for a sum due on account current with interest. These shares, although technically remaining under the control of the partners, meant the earnings for that proportion of the vessel were paid into an account with the mortgager, who charged interest on the amount outstanding, ensuring that if the capital sum of the mortgage was reduced the interest payable was reduced as a result. A further mortgage with Pickersgill's (*Bergamo* Mortgage "B") was taken out for another eight shares in the *Bergamo* on November 5, 1884. On that same day, a mortgage for 20 shares in the *Camargo* was negotiated by the partners with a friend and neighbour of Thomas, Miss Mary Elizabeth Jayne of 4 Clytha Square, Newport, and a further 27 shares with their mother in respect of the *Alassio.* A third mortgage (*Bergamo* Mortgage "C") was entered into in respect of that vessel with James Laing, William Stotart and John Crown, shipbuilders, on November 22, 1884. In relation to the three vessels, excluding the *Durango* which I will deal with shortly, the partners' shares were mortgaged as follows:—

Camargo—20 shares
Alassio—27 shares
Bergamo—47 shares

Basically there were two reasons for mortgaging their interests in these three ships. Having limited resources and undertaken the construction of the three ships, the third of the trio the *Durango* was financed by this means. This allowed the partners as their capital increased, to redeem their shares by the discharge of the mortgages. But more importantly, being merchants, they required large sums of working capital to enable them to finance their ever increasing transactions in relation to coal, iron ore and pitwood.

However, hardly had the *Durango* entered the fleet, than she became their first marine casualty when on November 27, 1884 she was sunk in the English Channel, South West of Dungeness in a collision with the barque *Luke Bruce* while on passage from Dunkirk to Genoa. This loss was a blow to Richard and Thomas, but rather than order a replacement, they decided to discharge all the mortgages in respect of their 47 shares in the *Bergamo,* which was accomplished within a matter of months.

With the arrival of these ships, it is interesting to note the appointment of Captain John Prance, a native of Braunton, Devon, as Master of the *Alassio*. Soon after, he was to take a single 64th share in the ship, starting his long association with Richard W. Jones and Company.

The three ships, *Camargo, Alassio* and *Bergamo* continued trading principally from Newport with coal to Gibraltar, Spain and Italy, returning with iron ore from Huelva usually to Garston.

During 1885 Captain Walter Runciman left the firm and early the following year entered shipowning on his own account at Newcastle. Captain Runciman was to become a major force in British Shipping in the coming years and the name Runciman is still to be found in the industry to the present day. His share in the *Camargo* passed to Richard himself on October 12, 1885.

During 1888 the partners decided to add a fourth ship to their fleet and ordered a 1,246 gross tons steamer from Wm. Pickersgill and Sons. Previously the ships had been constructed with iron hulls, but this ship, which was completed in January, 1889 as the *Ricardo* marked a departure from this as her hull was of steel.

From the Agreements and Accounts of the Crews it is possible to give details of the ports served by the Jones' ships for a sample of about one year. I will commence with the maiden voyage of the *Ricardo* which signed articles at South Shields on January 24, 1889.

S.S. *Ricardo*

VOYAGE DETAILS

24.1.1889—31.12.1889

Master: Captain John Prance until 31.5.1889
Captain John Say from 1.6.1889

South Shields—Huelva—Garston
Newport—Gibraltar—Huelva—Liverpool
Newport—Gibraltar—Newport
Newport—Gibraltar—Huelva—Garston
Swansea—Salerno—Huelva—Liverpool

Newport—Salerno—Carthagena—Gandia—Denia—Tabea—Almeria—London
Newport—Gibraltar—Huelva—Garston
Newport—Castellammane di Stabia—Huelva—Garston

S.S. *Bergamo*

VOYAGE DETAILS

23.7.1888—10.7.1889

Master: Captain W. L. Tremorrow

Liverpool—Newport—Gibraltar—Huelva—Garston
Penarth—Huelva—Liverpool
Newport—Gibraltar—Huelva—Garston
Newport—Gibraltar—Huelva—Liverpool
Newport—Gibraltar—Huelva—Liverpool
Newport—Gibraltar—Huelva—Liverpool
Newport—Gibraltar—Huelva—Liverpool
Penarth—Gibraltar—Carthagena—Tarragona—Burriana—Valencia—London
Newport—Gibraltar—Huelva—Liverpool
Newport—Huelva—Liverpool

S.S. *Camargo*

VOYAGE DETAILS

1.1.1889—8.7.1889

Master: Captain John Hy. Williams until 12.6.1889
Captain Jas. Williams from 12.6.1889

Liverpool—Newport—Huelva—Liverpool
Cardiff—Gibraltar—Huelva—Garston
Cardiff—Gibraltar—Huelva—Garston
Newport—Gibraltar—Carthagena—Burriana—Valencia—London
Newport—Gibraltar—Huelva—Birkenhead—Newport

S.S. *Alassio*

VOYAGE DETAILS

1.1.1889—31.12.1889

Master: Captain James Prance

Hull—Grimsby—Barcelona—Huelva—Hull
Grimsby—Gibraltar—Huelva—Garston
Newport—Gibraltar—Huelva—Hull
West Hartlepool—Aguilas—Huelva—Hull
Sunderland—Salerno—Huelva—Liverpool
Newport—Gibraltar—Huelva—Hull
Newcastle—Huelva—Garston
Cardiff—Penarth—Gibraltar—Huelva—Hull
Newcastle—South Shields—Huelva—Garston
Cardiff—Gibraltar—Huelva—Hull—Newcastle

In relation to coal exported from Newport in 1889 the following shows the ports to which the largest quantities were sent:—

Port	*Tonnage*
Genoa	199,308
Gibraltar	173,402
Bilbao	119,668
Lisbon	105,505
Malta	83,086
Buenos Aires	79,883
Las Palmas	78,654
Rio de Janeiro	72,325
Savona	62,357
Constantinople	60,405

Coal shipments during 1889 from Newport, including both the docks and river wharves, accounted for 2,129,568 tons foreign and 923,133 tons coastwise. These figures exclude bunker coal.

In relation to the masters of the ships, Captain John Prance was born in 1849 and now lived at Newport. His brother James, also a Devonian, was nine years older. Captain W. L. Tremorrow was a native of St. Ives, Cornwall who was born in 1843, while Captain John Say was born at Chester Le Street, Co. Durham in 1844, Captain Jas. Williams in 1848 at Westport, Mayo. Captain John Hy. Williams, the youngest of the firm's masters, was in fact the only Welshman and was born at Newport, Mon. in 1855.

In the following chapter I will endeavour to give details of some of the people who served on board the ships during some of the above mentioned voyages.

6. VOYAGE DETAILS OF S.S. "ALASSIO" 1.1.1889 TO 15.7.1889

At this stage I give details of a six month period of trading in relation to the *Alassio* during 1889, and a description of her crew. The *Alassio* had been in the fleet for a little over five years when she signed articles at Hull on January 1, 1889. Her crew of 19 was as follows:—

Rank	Name	Age	Place of Birth	Advance in Wages if Granted £ s. d.	Monthly Rate of Wages £ s. d.
Master	James Prance	49	Devon		not given
Mate	John Perkins	47	Pembroke		8 0 0
2nd Mate	C. F. Brown	22	Hull		5 15 0
Carpenter/ Seaman	Sam Perkis	48	St. John, N.B.		5 10 0
Cook	W. Cook	42	Tring		4 10 0
Steward	Wm. Whitting	29	Bridgwater		5 15 0
A.B./ Lamptrimmer	Antonio Phillips	35	Trieste, Italy		3 15 0
A.B.	Henry Johnson	30	Tonsberg, Norway		3 10 0
A.B.	William Craig	26	Londonderry		3 10 0
A.B.	James Stork	23	Hull	1 15 0	3 10 0
A.B.	H. Jonsson	28	Gothenburg Sweden	1 15 0	3 10 0
Engineer	Joseph Harrison	32	Liverpool		15 0 0
2nd Engineer	Geo. Mansfield	49	Cheltenham		10 0 0
Donkeyman/ Fireman	John Bloom	27	Stockholm, Sweden		4 10 0
Fireman	James Rossiter	36	Liverpool		3 15 0
Fireman	George Bailey	35	Hull		3 15 0
Fireman	John Walker	34	Nottingham	1 17 6	3 15 0
Fireman	Hern Kirk	31	Lubeck, Germany		3 15 0
Engineers' Steward	James Parkinson	18	Liverpool		1 10 0

Richard W. Jones and Company must have been a good employer and the ship popular with the crew, as nine of the above had been aboard the vessel the previous voyage. The Master, Captain James Prance, a brother of John Prance who was at that time standing by the new *Ricardo* which was fitting out at Sunderland, and the 1st Engineer, Joseph Harrison, had served on board the *Camargo* on their last voyage. Of the crew, six had been born abroad and indeed there was only one whose origin was in Wales, the Mate John Perkins from Pembroke. Bearing in mind that the vessel signed articles at Hull, this is not surprising, as the crews would be recruited locally at the signing on port, except for a nucleus of officers and petty officers. The ships sailing on six monthly articles meant that these ran out on a homeward leg of the last voyage and therefore the crew paid off at the first port on arrival. As the ships were at that time discharging usually at Garston or Hull, the crew changes were effected at this port, prior to sailing coastwise to the loading port, invariably Newport.

Most ships at that time on foreign going articles faced long voyages. But the Richard W. Jones and Company ships were back in the United Kingdom almost every month, at which time the crew could pay off if they wanted; another reason for the popularity of these ships could well be their short voyages.

Returning to the *Alassio,* she had discharged a cargo of iron ore at Hull and with the new articles having been opened, sailed for Grimsby in ballast where she loaded a full cargo of coal and set off for the Mediterranean, arriving at Barcelona on January 19. Her cargo took six days to unload. She then sailed back through the straits of Gibraltar to Huelva going alongside a loading berth on January 29 to load iron ore. Two days later she sailed for the United Kingdom, where once again her discharge port was Hull. On arrival two members of the crew paid off and left the vessel, as follows:—

Date	Rank	Name	Balance of Wages Paid
12.2.1889	A.B.	James Stork	2 14 8½
13.2.1889	Carpenter/A.B.	Sam Perkis	2 8 3½

Sam Perkis was a regular on Richard W. Jones' vessels and was highly thought of. Less than two weeks later, on February 26 he signed on board the new *Ricardo* at Garston for a voyage which was to end on May 31; he was with Captain John Prance with whom he had previously served. On February 14 a new carpenter/seaman was signed on the *Alassio* at Hull, and having left for Grimsby to load her cargo of coal, a replacement A.B. joined.

Rank	Name	Age	Place of Birth	Advance in Wages if Granted £	s.	d.	Monthly Rate of Wages £	s.	d.
Carpenter/ A.B.	John Morris	42	Hull	2	15	0	5	10	0
A.B.	Samuel May	36	Brixham	1	7	6	3	15	0

She left Grimsby on February 15 for Gibraltar where she arrived on February 24. Her cargo was discharged and she sailed on March 2 for Huelva to load the inevitable cargo of iron ore. Nine days later she sailed for Garston where the following crew members were paid of:—

Date	Rank	Name	Balance of Wages Paid
19.3.1889	Fireman	James Rossiter	1 1 3½
19.3.1889	Fireman	George Bailey	19 6
19.3.1889	Fireman	John Walker	2 4 6
21.3.1889	A.B./Lamptrimmer	Antonio Phillips	4 9 6
21.3.1889	A.B.	Henry Johnson	3 15 11
21.3.1889	A.B.	William Craig	3 16 1½
21.3.1889	A.B.	H. Jonsson	3 15 4
21.3.1889	Engineers' Steward	James Parkinson	1 17 0
22.3.1889	Carpenter/Seaman	John Morris	4 0 2½
22.3.1889	Fireman	Hern Kirk	2 6
25.3.1889	2nd Engineer	Geo. Mansfield	0

The new crew members were signed on, three of whom had changed their minds and re-signed articles. The new 2nd Engineer, having recently qualified, had previously served as 3rd Engineer on the *Bergamo*. The monthly wage rate quoted below for A.B.'s and Firemen had been increased by 5/- per month, whereas the new carpenter/seaman's rate had gone down from £5 10s. 0d. to £5, probably because he was a newcomer to the firm.

Rank	Name	Age	Place of Birth	Advance in Wages if Granted £	s.	d.	Monthly Rate of Wages £	s.	d.
21.3.1889									
Fireman	Tom Shaw Armstrong	41	Newhaven	2	0	0	4	0	0
Fireman	Arthur Rainey	40	Belfast	2	0	0	4	0	0
Fireman	Joseph Pierce	27	Liverpool	2	0	0	4	0	0
22.3.1889									
A.B./ Lamptrimmer	Antonio Phillips	35	Trieste, Italy				4	0	0
A.B.	H. Jonsson	28	Gothenburg, Sweden				3	15	0
23.3.1889									
Fireman	Hern Kirk	31	Lubeck, Germany				4	0	0
A.B.	George Olsen	22	Norway				3	15	0
25.3.1889									
Carpenter/ A.B.	James McGibbon	31	West Indies				5	0	0
A.B.	John Byrne	42	Arklow				3	15	0
Engineers' Steward	Richard Atkin	15	Liverpool				1	10	0
26.3.1889									
2nd Engineer	Chris Elliott	23	Gateshead				10	0	0

The ship sailed on March 26 in ballast for Newport where a cargo of coal was loaded. The mate signed off on April 1 with a balance of wages of 16/- and then re-signed articles the following day. The ship sailed for Gibraltar, arriving on April 11, proceeded to Huelva and then back to Hull with iron ore. There were no crew changes at this port and she proceeded to West Hartlepool to load coal. At this port, the A.B./Lamptrimmer was replaced.

6.5.1889 Paid Off:

Rank	Name	Balance of Wages Paid £	s.	d.
A.B./Lamptrimmer	Antonio Phillips		8	0

7.5.1889 Signed on:

Rank	Name	Age	Place of Birth	Advance in Wages if Granted £	s.	d.	Monthly Rate of Wages £	s.	d.
A.B./ Lamptrimmer	George Prance	21	Newport				4	0	0

The latter was a relative of the master, probably his son. The ship sailed on May 11 for Aguilas, where she arrived two weeks later and took a week to unload. She then proceeded to Huelva, loaded iron ore, and then started out for Hull, where on arrival the following were paid off on June 7.

Rank	Name	Balance of Wages Paid £	s.	d.
Mate	John Perkins	8	7	9
Carpenter/A.B.	Wm. McGibbon	4	14	8
A.B.	Samuel May	3	18	0
A.B.	H. Jonsson	3	3	0
Engineers' Steward	Richard Atkin	1	9	9½

The next day three crew members were signed on:—

Rank	Name	Age	Place of Birth	Advance in Wages if Granted £	s.	d.	Monthly Rate of Wages £	s.	d.
Mate	Griffith Morris	50	Caernarvon				8	0	0
A.B.	Frank Kennedy	39	Dorset	2	2	6	4	5	0
A.B.	Victor Johnson	48	Finland	2	2	6	4	5	0

Having unloaded her cargo of ore, the *Alassio* sailed in ballast for Sunderland with two crew members short and on June 11 six more men were paid off.

Rank	Name	Balance of Wages Paid £ s. d.
Engineer	J. Harrison	1 0 0
Donkeyman/ Fireman	John Bloom	6 0
Fireman	Tom Shaw Armstrong	5 4
Fireman	Arthur Rainey	5 4
Fireman	Joseph Pierce	5 4
Fireman	Hern Kirk	2 8

On the same day, the following were signed on, four of whom had only just signed off. The monthly rate of wages had increased by 10/- in respect of petty officers, A.B.'s and firemen. The carpenter/A.B. Sam Perkis, after his absence in the *Ricardo*, rejoined the vessel.

Rank	Name	Age	Place of Birth	Advance in Wages if Granted £ s. d.	Monthly Rate of Wages £ s. d.
Carpenter/ A.B.	Sam Perkis	49	St. John's, N.B.		5 10 0
Donkeyman/ Fireman	John Bloom	27	Stockholm		5 10 0
Fireman	Tom Shaw Armstrong	41	Whitehaven		4 10 0
Fireman	Joseph Pierce	27	Liverpool		4 10 0
Fireman	Arthur Rainey	49	Belfast		4 10 0
Engineers' Steward	Geo. Robinson	16	Sunderland		1 10 0

On June 12 the able seaman Frank Kennedy who had signed on the *Alassio* at Hull four days earlier deserted. He had been granted an advance in wages of £2 2s. 6d. and having only served on the ship for four days thus provided a deficit which could not be recovered. Further crew members were signed on at Sunderland on June 12.

Rank	Name	Age	Place of Birth	Advance in Wages if Granted £ s. d.	Monthly Rate of Wages £ s. d.
Engineer	John Prosser	67	Abergavenny		15 0 0
Fireman	Hern Kirk	32	Lubeck		4 10 0
A.B.	Robert Purvis	23	Whitburn		4 5 0

Having signed on at the Mercantile Marine Office, A.B. Robert Purvis failed to join the ship and as a result the following day a replacement was engaged:—

Rank	Name	Age	Place of Birth	Advance in Wages if Granted £ s. d.	Monthly Rate of Wages £ s. d.
A.B.	Arthur Smith	24	London	3 0 0	4 5 0

The replacement Chief Engineer is of great interest as he was born at Abergavenny as far back as 1822, making him an early engineer in the development of the steamship. He signed his name in the Welsh style with the first letter "s" being more in the way of an "f". He was really, at 67 years of age, more of a relief engineer, serving in the firm's ships as and when required, but obviously not wanting to sail continuously; he had last served on the *Bergamo* between December 18, 1888 and January 19, 1889. The German fireman Hern Kirk, had in fact re-signed articles.

After loading her cargo of coal, the ship sailed for the Italian port of Salerno where she arrived on June 25, took three days to discharge and then left for Huelva for the customary cargo of iron ore to be taken on board. She set off for the United Kingdom arriving at Liverpool on July 15, where the entire crew paid off as the ship's articles had run out.

Rank	Name	Balance of Wages Paid £	s.	d.
Master	James Prance	Remained in Vessel		
Mate	Griffith Morris	5	12	5
2nd Mate	C. F. Brown	7	1	7½
Carpenter/A.B.	Sam Perkis	1	18	8
Cook	W. Cook		12	3
Steward	Wm. Whitting	1	13	2½
A.B.	George Olsen	4	13	6
A.B.	John Byrne	4	8	3
A.B.	Victor Johnson	2	18	0
A.B.	Arthur Smith	1	13	10
Engineer	John Prosser	17	9	9½
2nd Engineer	Chris Elliott	12	6	5½
Donkeyman/ Fireman	John Bloom	2	8	4
Fireman	Tom Shaw Armstrong		18	9½
Fireman	Joseph Pierce	1	11	10
Fireman	Arthur Rainey	1	6	9
Fireman	Hern Kirk	4	19	4½
Engineers' Steward	Geo. Robinson		18	7

Including the Master, six members of the ship's compliment had been in the vessel throughout the 6½ months and the Carpenter/A.B. had been in the ship earlier in the articles. The ship signed articles again at Liverpool on July 16, and it is interesting to note that the Master and twelve of the crew re-signed, there only being six newcomers to the ship.

The following extracts are taken from the ship's articles for the voyage described above:—

SCALE OF PROVISIONS

Scale of Provisions to be allowed and served out to the Crew during the Voyage, in addition to the daily issue of Lime and Lemon Juice and Sugar, or other antiscorbutics in any case required by 30th & 31st Vict., c. 124 s.4.

At the rate of:

DAILY

Bread 1lb; Tea $\frac{1}{8}$oz; Coffee $\frac{1}{2}$oz; Sugar 2oz; Water 3 qts.

Every Sunday, Tuesday, Thursday, Saturday

Beef $1\frac{1}{2}$lb.

Every Monday, Wednesday, Friday

Pork $1\frac{1}{4}$lb; Peas $\frac{1}{4}$ pint.

Every Sunday, Tuesday, Thursday

Flour $\frac{1}{2}$lb.

Every Saturday

Rice $\frac{1}{2}$lb.

NOTE: In any case an equal quantity of Fresh Meat or Fresh Vegetables may at the option of the Master, be served out in lieu of the Salted or Tinned Meats or Preserved or Compressed Vegetables named in the above Scale.

SUBSTITUTES

At the Master's Option No Spirits Allowed

The ship's crew must have been reasonably satisfied with their food as they came back in many cases for voyage after voyage.

Other extracts from the ship's articles (Agreement and Account of Crew) of a Foreign-Going Ship are as follows:—

THE SEVERAL PERSONS whose names are hereto subscribed, and whose descriptions are contained on the other side or sides, and of whom FIVE are engaged as Sailors, hereby agree to serve on board the said Ship in the several capacities expressed against their respective Names, on a Voyage from:—

Hull to Grimsby thence Barcelona or/and any Ports or places within the limits of 30 and 70 degrees North Latitude trading in Coasting, Home or Foreign trades: term not to extend beyond the 30th June next or the first arrival of the ship at her port of destination in the United Kingdom after such date, or the discharge of cargo consequent upon such arrival.

And the Crew agree to conduct themselves in an orderly, faithful, honest, and sober manner, and to be at all times diligent in their respective duties, and to be obedient to the lawful commands of the said Master, or of any Person who shall lawfully succeed him, and of their Superior Officers, in everything relating to the said Ship and the Stores and Cargo thereof, whether on board, in boats, or on shore: in consideration of which Services to be duly performed, the said Master hereby agrees to pay to the said Crew as Wages the Sums against their Names respectively expressed, and to supply them with Provisions according to the above Scale. And it is hereby agreed, That any Embezzlement or wilful or negligent Destruction of any part of the Ship's Cargo or Stores shall be made good to the Owner out of the Wages of the Person guilty of the same: And if any Person enters himself as qualified for a duty which he proves incompetent to perform, his Wages shall be reduced in proportion to his incompetency: And it is also agreed, That the Regulations authorised by the Board of Trade, which are printed herein and numbered 1 to 4

are adopted by the parties hereto, and shall be considered as embodied in this Agreement: And it is also agreed, That if any Member of the Crew considers himself to be aggrieved by any breach of the Agreement or otherwise, he shall represent the same to the Master or Officer in charge of the Ship in a quiet and orderly manner, who shall thereupon take such steps as the case may require. And it is also agreed, That the said Master shall be entitled to deduct from the wages of the said Crew respectively the following amounts, viz,:— for not joining at the time specified in Column 10, two days' pay, or any expenses which have been properly incurred in hiring a substitute—and for absence from the Ship at any time without leave, a sum not exceeding two weeks' pay; and it is hereby mutually agreed, that any dispute arising on the subject of these deductions shall be settled by the Superintendent of a Mercantile Marine Office, Consular Officer, or Shipping Master abroad, and that his decision shall be final. And it is also agreed, That

The Master may discharge any of the Crew, in the United Kingdom, without notice, as circumstances in his opinion may require.

Twenty four hours' notice on the part of the crew may terminate this agreement at a port in the United Kingdom.
No cash shall be advanced abroad or liberty granted other than at the pleasure of the Master.
The Seamen and Firemen shall mutually assist each other in the general duties of the ship.
Should any of the Crew fail to join at the time specified, the Master may ship substitutes at once.
In the event of detention by Ice, the Master shall have the option of sending any part of the Crew back to the Port of

Delivered to Richard W. Jones and Company in 1883 the "Alassio" had been built by the Strand Slipway Company, Sunderland. The ship is shown aground in the Humber. (K. O.'Donoghue.)

The "Elorrio" joined the fleet in 1894 from the Sunderland yard of Wm. Pickersgill and Sons.
(York Collection.)

The first "Uskmouth" was built in 1916 by J. Priestman and Company, Sunderland.
(National Maritime Museum.)

Acquired in 1921 from other owners the "Uskside (2) had been built four years earlier by Craig, Taylor and Co. Ltd., Stockton. (A. Duncan.)

The "Uskside" (2) remained in the fleet until 1931. (York Collection.)

One of seven steamers built for the firm by the Burntisland Shipbuilding Co. Ltd., the "Uskbridge" (1) was delivered in 1924. (World Ship Photo Library.)

The first "Uskbridge" heavily laden with esparto grass. (A. Duncan.)

The first "Uskport" entered the fleet of the Uskport Steamship Co. Ltd. in 1925.
(York Collection.)

The steamer "Uskport" of 1925. (A. Duncan.)

A striking view of the "Uskmouth" (2) which was delivered to the Uskside Steamship Co. Ltd. in 1928.
(National Maritime Museum.)

The "Uskvalley" of 1929. (National Maritime Museum.)

Launch Party for the "Uskside" (3) at Burntisland on November 26, 1936. The ship was launched by Mrs. Sara Rainforth.

The "Uskside" (3) enters the water at Burntisland on November 26, 1936.

Launch Party at Burntisland for the "Uskbridge" of 1940. From the left: Guy Treverton Jones, Lady Ayre, Mrs. Joyce Treverton Jones (who launched the ship), and Sir Amos Ayre.

Built in 1944 as the "Empire Osborne" the second "Uskport" joined the fleet in 1946.
(Skyfotos Ltd.)

The "Uskport" in the English Channel on passage from North Africa to the Firth of Forth with a cargo of esparto grass

departure in the United Kingdom at the expense of the Owners, the stipulations relating to wages and provisions remaining in force up to the time of arrival.

IN WITNESS whereof the said parties have subscribed their Names on the other Side or Sides hereof on the days against their respective Signatures mentioned.

Signed by JAMES PRANCE Master,
on the 1st day of Jan., 1889.

A very comprehensive document, but I note that in a number of cases the crew members were unable to read or write as they made their mark rather than signing. However, the Mercantile Marine Superintendent inserted the name of the man, when this was the case.

Desertions amongst the crews varied. Alcohol in port was a problem, as a number failed to join at the time of sailing, or plain deserted or as referred to by seamen "Jumped Ship".

On July 18, 1889 two firemen, Jas. Farrell aged 27 and Charles Webster aged 21, of Liverpool and Birkenhead respectively, failed to join the *Alassio* at Liverpool, having signed articles two days earlier. On October 14 of the same year fireman C. V. Smith, aged 28 of Belfast, deserted (not on board vessel at time of sailing) at Huelva, and the ship sailed without him. When located by the authorities, he would have been returned home at the direction of the British Vice-Consulate as a Distressed British Seaman on board the next British flag merchant vessel to call at the port. An imposition not negotiable by the Master of the ship. This fireman had previously served on board the *Camargo*. On October 28 fireman J. Muff aged 22 of Hull, deserted from the *Alassio* at Hull after five days on board and on October 30 at South Shields, fireman James Skelly 27 years, of that port failed to join the ship. To list all the desertions from the ships during 1888/1889 would take too much space, but one worth mentioning is fireman Wm. Cliffard, aged 33 of Garston. On September 3, 1888 he deserted from the *Bergamo* at Garston; surprisingly he was to complete a voyage on that ship between May 23 and July 10, 1889. However, on November 21, of that year he deserted from the *Ricardo* at Newport, having joined that ship a few days earlier at Garston.

The most fascinating entry I have found in the ship's articles for 1889 is the entry for A. T. Jones, aged 11 years of Newport, who signed on the *Bergamo* at Newport on June 18, 1889 as a cabin boy at the monthly rate of 1/- for a voyage under the command of Captain W. L. Tremorrow to Gibraltar and Huelva and paid off at Garston on July 10. This was the son of the partner's younger brother Bonn. The 11 year old boy, Alan Treverton Jones, who was later to become involved in the business, was signed on the Ship's Articles as was the partner's custom when a junior member of the family went on a voyage, to firmly put him under the control of the Master. In the years to come, a number of younger members of the family were to spend voyages on the firm's ships during their holidays in order to expand their experience. In effect the wage of 1/- per month was that of a supernumerary.

7. THE DEATH OF RICHARD WILLIAM JONES AND RESULTING REORGANISATION

By 1890 the partnership of Richard W. Jones and Company had become well established as one of Newport's most successful merchant houses. Richard and Thomas were involved with Newport Harbour Commissioners and the Newport Shipowners' Association and their influence had grown. They were leading merchants in respect of the export of coal, the importation of iron ore and pit props and with ten years' experience in the operation of their own ships were taking full advantage of the expanding trade through the port. In 1875 the business had moved offices from 70 to 75 Dock Street, and in 1891 was to move to larger premises at No. 112.

However, on April 26, 1890 a major blow befell the business, when Richard William Jones died suddenly at the age of 47. Thomas was in the position of having to take control of the business, to introduce his youngest brother into the partnership and to extricate his late brother's capital on behalf of his widow Helen, who, not having any of her five children involved in the venture, wished to withdraw the capital. With Richard's death, Thomas had to discharge their joint mortgages in respect of the ships and whilst I have not been able to inspect the registers for all of them, I give the following details in respect of those I have.

On July 21 of that year therefore, the mortgage in respect of the *Camargo* for 20 shares with Mary Elizabeth Jayne of 4 Clytha Square, was discharged and together with the 11 shares which had passed back to the partners prior to Richard's death, this accounted for 31 shares. Immediately Thomas transferred three shares to Bonn and the one share held by Richard on his own, was sold by his widow to Bonn. This meant that there was no longer any mortgage in respect of the *Camargo* and Thomas now held 28 shares and Bonn four shares in the vessel.

At the same time, the mortgage in respect of 27 shares of the *Alassio* with the partner's mother was discharged. A new one was taken out by Thomas on his own, for 20 shares in respect of this ship with the family's good friend Miss Jayne. The *Bergamo* which had previously been free from mortgage, was then committed by Thomas for a mortgage in respect of 40 shares with his mother. Thomas by these various transactions managed to restructure the business and at the same time withdraw his late brother's capital. It obviously stretched his resources, but the increased involvement by his mother for 40 shares in the *Bergamo* as opposed to the previous mortgage for 27 in the *Alassio* helped to achieve this. The mortgage, in effect transferred from *Camargo* to *Alassio* for 20 shares with Miss Jayne, left the capital more or less the same. Bonn's introduction as a shareholder in the ships at this stage further eased the situation for Thomas. Regarding the *Ricardo,* I have no details.

The difficulties in withdrawing from the business an estimated half of its capital reflected highly on Thomas' ability as a businessman, as a lesser man would probably have had to wind up the venture. However, he had now become a major shareholder in many ways by mortgages in the fleet of ships. Whereas in the past, the shares in the ships were held jointly by Thomas and Richard, this method had now ceased as Thomas had more capital than his younger brother Bonn and their holdings were kept distinctly separate. However, in respect of earnings from the partnership of Richard W. Jones and Company, by way of activities as merchants and fees in respect of the management of the ships, they shared as equals. Thus the shares, which had in the past been held by the partnership, were now separate from it. Bonn had in fact spent a number of years in the firm's offices previously, but in the capacity of an employee undertaking the duties of a clerk.

Hardly had the new arrangements been completed, when they suffered their second marine loss. The steamer *Ricardo,* which was only two years old, was lost on April 10, 1891 near Cape St. Mary after a collision with the vessel *Adelphi Couppa,* on passage with a cargo of iron ore from Huelva to the Mersey. Thomas and Bonn decided not to replace her and concentrated their energy in trading the three remaining steamers *Alassio, Bergamo* and *Camargo.*

On November 3, 1893 their pioneer vessel *Camargo,* after 13 years in the fleet, was also lost by collision, this time with the steamer *Biscaye* in the Bristol Channel off Sully Island while on passage coastwise in ballast to Newport.

With the sinking of the *Camargo,* the partners wasted no time in negotiating with Wm. Pickersgill and Sons, Sunderland, for the construction of a replacement. The contract for this ship, designated yard number 104, was signed on December 26 and she was launched as the *Elorrio* on June 2, 1894, and delivered to Richard W. Jones and Company on July 26. She was of 1,347 gross tons, had a steel hull and like the earlier steamers owned by the partners was of the raised quarter deck type.

The connections between the partners and coal importers in Spain and Italy were further developed during this period. The partners were individually Vice-Consuls at Newport in respect of a number of foreign governments, including Italy and Denmark.

In 1897 they decided to sell the *Bergamo* and concentrate more on their activities as merchants. As a result, on May 5 of that year she passed to Norwegian owners and traded under that flag, although changing owners several times, until October 24, 1908 when she was wrecked at Thornton-Lock, Innerwick, on passage London to Grangemouth in ballast. The mortgage for 40 shares in this ship with his mother, Anne Eliza Jones, was discharged by Thomas just prior to the sale, though she was to continue to hold an interest in the ships by taking 64th shares in the normal way.

The fleet was to remain at two ships for well over a decade. Both Thomas and Bonn felt that it was better sense to concentrate their resources in what was still their main activity as merchants. At least half of their time was being spent on the floor of the Cardiff Coal Exchange negotiating the purchase of coal on behalf of their foreign clients and chartering tonnage where needed. Their own ships, when on voyage charters, were fixed by the partners on the Exchange.

Meanwhile, in relation to the growth of Newport as a sea port, in 1882 the original Newport Dock Company and the Alexandra (Newport) Dock Company amalgamated and became the Alexandra (Newport and South Wales) Docks and Railway Company. The expansion of world trade continued unchecked and the new company embarked on the construction of an additional dock, the Alexandra South Dock with a deep water area of 38.85 hectares. This was constructed in three stages, the Northern section comprising 8.09 hectares with an entrance lock 21.95 metres wide was opened in June, 1893 followed by the 19.43 hectare southern portion in 1907 and third and final section of 11.33 hectares, including the South Lock Entrance, was completed in 1914.

The total tonnage handled at Newport Docks (not including the berths in the River Usk) had increased from 2,422,619 tons in 1880 to 4,604,549 tons in 1899; coal and coke shipments accounting for figures of 1,449,050 tons and 3,999,537 tons respectively.

8. VOYAGE DETAILS OF S.S, "ALASSIO" 18.7.1898 TO 2.7.1899

The following list of ports visited by the *Alassio* between July 18, 1898 and July 3, 1899 reflects a slight reduction in the shipments to the coaling station at Gibraltar and consequent increase to Spain and Italy. The iron ore shipped at Huelva was being carried more often to the North East Coast or South Wales ports, as opposed to Garston, a decade earlier.

S.S. *Alassio*

VOYAGE DETAILS

18.7.1898—3.7.1899

Master: Captain John Prance

Hull—Goole—Sunderland—Castellion—Huelva—Liverpool
Newport—Lisbon—Huelva—London—Goole
Newport—Gibraltar—Huelva—Swansea
Newport—Gibraltar—Huelva—Hull—Ipswich
Newport—Salerno—Huelva—Hull
Newport—Gibraltar—Huelva—Hull—Goole
Newport—Gibraltar—Huelva—Swansea
Newport—Gibraltar—Huelva—Port Talbot
Newport—Gibraltar—Huelva—Hull—Goole—Newport

As a result of the ships' discharging more often in South Wales ports, an increasing number of Welshmen or men who had made their homes in South Wales were serving in the Jones' ships. This is illustrated by the crew who signed on the *Alassio* at Hull on July 18, 1898 most of whom had served on the vessel on the previous voyage. The articles now included the address of the crew member and was explained thus:

1. Port of Engagement Address, and
2. Home Address

N.B. Both to be inserted. The Home Address is the one to which communications should be made in the event of the death of the Seaman.

In practice, only section 2 was usually filled in, but where a second entry in the articles is made I have shown it in the list of crew:—

Rank	Name	Age	Birthplace	Address
Master	John Prance	49	Devon	7 Alma St., Newport
Mate	Richard F. G. Byddu	30	Glamorgan	St. Georges Cottage, Port Talbot, Glam.
2nd Mate	George Phillips	45	Swansea	13 Clarence Terr., Swansea

Rank	Name	Age	Birthplace	Address
Cook	D. Clark	50	Hayle	Market Place, Hayle
Steward	P. Strange	64	Swansea	11 Clarence Terr., Swansea
A.B./ Lamptrimmer	Alfred Rothman	38	Nystadt, Finland	1. 18 Paradise Pl., Hull 2. Nystadt, Finland
A.B.	Charles Rush	33	Wexford	9 Shakespeare St., Garston
A.B.	Victor Danielson	24	Carlsund	Carlsund, Sweden
A.B.	Pitter Vopke	34	Helsingborg, Sweden	3 Shand, Swansea
A.B.	Thomas White	39	Folkestone	3 Broadley Sq., Hull
A.B.	Gustav Linde	23	Bergen, Norway	26 Nile St., Hull
1st Engineer	John Smith	44	Tunstall	Martins Bank, Falke, Nr. Stoke
2nd Engineer	John C. Smith	22	Cheshire	Martins Bank, Falke, Nr. Stoke
Donkeyman	Jonathan Thomas	55	Newport	33 Nelson St., Newport
Fireman	Ahmed Mahomed	35	Constantinople	11 Kemble St., Swansea
Fireman	Joseph Jones	28	Swansea	24 Caepistyll St., Swansea
Fireman	John Standen	27	Southwick	28 Hafford St., Swansea
Fireman	John Dunn	35	Newport	6 Price St., Newport
Engineers' Steward	Bernard McGuire	17	Goole	26 George St., Goole

Monthly wage rates were as follows:—

	£	s.	d.
Master	Not given		
Mate	8	0	0
2nd Mate	6	0	0
Cook	5	10	0
Steward	6	0	0
A.B./Lamptrimmer	4	5	0
A.B.'s	4	0	0
1st Engineer	15	0	0
2nd Engineer	10	0	0
Donkeyman	5	0	0
Firemen	4	5	0
Engineers' Steward	2	0	0

These rates showed a decrease of 5/- for firemen and seamen (A.B.'s) and an increase of 10/- for the engineer's steward by comparison with wages nine years earlier. When the ship re-signed articles on January 31, 1899 at Hull, the rates remained unchanged except for the A.B./Lamptrimmer whose wages per month had increased by 12/6d. to £4 17s. 6d; A.B.'s increased by 12/6 to £4 12s. 6d; Donkeymen 7/6 to £5 7s. 6d; and firemen up 7/6 to £4 12s. 6d. The rates for A.B.'s and firemen had by now become the same. However, there were clearly fluctuations from year to year, if not even voyage to voyage. In difficult times, wages were reduced in respect of seamen, firemen and petty officers, but there is no evidence that the officers shared in these reductions.

The crew signed on at Hull on January 31, 1899 was as follows:—

Rank	Name	Age	Birthplace	Address
Master	John Prance	50	Braunton, Devon	7 Alma St., Newport
Mate	Richard F. G. Byddu	31	Taibach, S/Wales	Port Talbot, Glamorgan
2nd Mate	John Corrin	50	Liverpool	32 Brackfield Rd., Liverpool
Steward	E. C. Poole	49	Gloucester	90 Durham Rd., Newport
Cook	R. Burke	38	Jamaica	Kingston, Jamaica
A.B./ Lamptrimmer	Alfred Rothman	39	Nystadt, Finland	17 Paradise Pl., Hull
A.B.	Charles Knott	40	Everton	53 Lime St., Newport
A.B.	Gustav Linde	24	Bergen, Norway	Bergen, Norway
A.B.	W. McNamara	39	Cork	1 Wolsley St., Newport
A.B.	W. Schulz	39	Hamburg	Hamburg, Germany
A.B.	T. Wolff	24	Kiel	Kiel, Germany
1st Engineer	John Smith	44	Tunstall	Martins Bank, Falke, Nr. Stoke
2nd Engineer	John C. Smith	23	Cheshire	Martins Bank, Falke, Nr. Stoke
Donkeyman	Jonathan Thomas	56	Newport	36 Hewetson St., Newport
Fireman	Joseph Jones	29	Swansea	24 Caepistyll St., Swansea
Fireman	John Dunn	36	Newport	6 Price St., Newport
Fireman	Garrett Mahoney	31	Newport	33 Hewetson St., Newport
Fireman	John Jones	32	Manchester	39 Daniel St., Seacombe
Engineer's Steward	Hockmann	19	Hamburg	Hamburg, Germany

Again, a percentage of the crew, six out of nineteen were of foreign origin; but there were a clear number, nine, who were of Welsh origin or were resident in South Wales.

9. DEATH OF THOMAS JONES, CONTROL OF THE BUSINESS PASSES TO BONN HENRY JONES

The founder's mother, although her role had ended as a mortgagor in the ships, had continued to support the venture by taking shares in them. However, on March 6, 1901 she died. Her support for her family had continued for twenty years after the death of her husband and she had played an important part in the financing of the business, particularly following the death of Richard in 1890.

Unfortunately, on October 18, 1903 the surviving founder partner, Thomas, died, leaving a big gap which his brother Bonn, now aged fifty, had to fill. The shares in the ships which had been held by Thomas passed to his widow, Annie Jane Wilson Jones, on his death and in the case of the *Alassio,* amounted to 21/64ths. Bonn, who had married Kate Oliver of Cornwall, had three sons, Alan Treverton Jones, Godfrey Treverton Jones and Guy Treverton Jones and early in 1903 both Alan, who was aged 26 and Guy who was 22, had each taken one share in the *Alassio*. However, with the death of Thomas, Bonn had to find the capital to buy out Thomas' share, a difficult task. The ships were now free from mortgages and on November 7, 1904 Bonn was able to take the 21 shares in the *Alassio* from Mrs. Jones who was by now living at "Clytha", Cambridge, Waikato, New Zealand and the transaction was attended to by her solicitor John Atkinson, to whom she had given power of attorney on June 1.

I do not know the number of shares involved in respect of the *Elorrio,* but the 21 in the *Alassio* were apportioned 17 to Bonn and two each to Alan and Guy, making Bonn's holding 38 and his sons four each. Godfrey who did not enter the business had emigrated to Canada and was farming in Calgary.

The partnership of Richard W. Jones and Company, now in Bonn's hands, needed a second partner; thus Guy was admitted. Guy had been involved in the office since leaving school at 18. However, Alan although taking the shares mentioned previously, was an architect, and did not actually become a partner in the business until several years had elapsed.

The two ships continued trading, and Bonn, who apparently had little aptitude for business, introduced Guy to the floor of the Cardiff Coal Exchange, where they continued to negotiate the purchase of coal on behalf of their long standing contacts in Spain and Italy. When not carrying coal on their own behalf, the ships were fixed on charter on the Exchange.

Bonn was a well known local figure, much respected for his support of charitable institutions and was not fired by any great ambitions unlike his two departed brothers. He was content to make a living for himself and his family, and gained more enjoyment and pleasure from his activities outside the business than in it. It was in this setting that Guy and later Alan, commenced their training in the business.

Gradually Bonn had increased his holding of shares in the two ships and in the case of the *Alassio* had by 1905 secured 48, whilst Alan and Guy still had four each. The outstanding eight shares were held one each by the following:—

Henry Ernest Baddeley
William Denton
William Tattersall
Albert Augustus Newman
Thomas Proctor
Robert Arthur Moorhouse
Emily Warren
Elizabeth Swarbrick and John Charnley, jointly.

At this time it was decided to register the two remaining ships, *Alassio* and *Elorrio*, in the ownership of single ship companies, and in consequence on January 17, 1906, the Alassio Steamship Co. Ltd. and the Elorrio Steamship Co. Ltd. were formed, of which Richard W. Jones and Company were managers. The 64 shares in each ship held by the family and others were converted into shareholdings in the new companies and the profits were thereafter distributed to the shareholders in proportion to their holdings. The partnership continued to maintain offices and staff. They undertook the chartering and other matters appertaining to the ships and received a management fee from the owning companies.

Previously, under the old 64 share system there was no limit to the liability which could be incurred by the shareholders in the ships. If, for instance, a judgement was made against the ship in respect of a collision for which the Master was adjudged responsible, the resulting claim would be divided against the 64 shares. This could be a risky business, thus the more sensible and realistic registration of limited liability companies, restricted the liability to the share capital of the company. With this system a claim in respect of one ship could not be made against the other, as they were owned by completely separate companies.

10. FORMATION OF THE USKSIDE STEAMSHIP CO. LTD.

The *Alassio* and *Elorrio* continued trading, but in 1910 and coinciding with a Dock Strike at Newport, it was decided to sell the older ship, which had by now been in the fleet for 27 years. The *Alassio* passed to Swedish owners and was to remain afloat until 1953, when she arrived at Gateshead for breaking up, having completed seventy years in service, a true testimony to British shipbuilding. At the time the ship was disposed of, the owning company was wound up.

This left the *Elorrio* trading alone, but by now Bonn was under pressure from his sons Guy and Alan to expand their interests particularly in shipping. Bonn resisted, preferring to keep the business at a size which provided an adequate livelihood for him and his sons, while not involving him with the problems associated with a large venture. However the brothers persisted and pursuaded their father that the time was right to replace the 1,347 gross ton *Elorrio* with a new larger ship. Thus, on October 15, 1912 a new company was incorporated with a capital of £5,000 made up of 50 shares of £100 each. This company, the Uskside Steamship Co. Ltd., took its name from the River Usk, the West bank of which was only a very short distance from the firm's offices. At this time an order was placed with J. Priestman and Company of Sunderland, for a steamer of 2,066 gross tons, which was duly delivered the following year as the *Uskside*. From then the practice was adopted of naming all subsequent ships with the well-known "Usk" prefix—hence the title of this volume.

With the arrival of the *Uskside,* the *Elorrio* was sold to foreign interests, but she, like the *Alassio,* was to have a long career before arriving at Dunston on February 12, 1954 for breaking up. With this ship's sale, the Elorrio Steamship Co. Ltd., was wound up.

The new company was managed by the partnership and at the outbreak of the First World War they were still a single ship company. Bonn, being a true patriot, immediately offered his new ship to the Admiralty and, as a result, three weeks after the start of hostilities and having arrived back from a voyage to the Mediterranean and discharged her cargo of iron ore, she was requisitioned by the Admiralty for service as a fleet collier. Although still owned by the Uskside Steamship Co. Ltd., the ship came under the complete control of the Admiralty, who paid a monthly sum for her use. This sum was adequate, but was as nothing compared with her earnings potential if she had remained under the management of Richard W. Jones and Company, as the full control of the movements and cargoes in relation to all British merchant ships was not undertaken until 1917, when the British Government appointed a Shipping Controller. This meant that vast fortunes were to be made with the operation of ships for the first three years of the war, Bonn's commendable attitude in actual fact depriving the business of some handsome returns.

During the early part of the war, the two younger partners pursuaded their father to agree to order another steamer, which was delivered from J. Priestman and Company, Sunderland, in 1916 as the *Uskmouth.* This ship was employed on commercial service mostly to the Mediterranean and came under the directions of the Shipping Controller from 1917, although unlike her consort *Uskside,* she remained under the management of Richard W. Jones and Company.

On April 8, 1918 the *Uskside* was attacked by a submarine in the North Sea, which fired a torpedo which fortunately missed. The partners in view of this, decided to sell her even though she was still in service as an Admiralty collier. She was really a valuable asset and would have fetched in the region of £100,000, approximately four times the cost of building her five years earlier. Thus a substantial reserve of capital was secured, which, as will be shown later, was used to good effect after the war.

The *Uskside* passed to other British owners, who renamed her *Largo* and in 1919 was released by the Admiralty and returned to commercial service under her new owners. In 1946 she passed to National Chinese owners. She was last heard of in 1952 when she was reported to have had engine trouble and presumably was broken up soon after.

11. ENTRY INTO THE ESPARTO TRADE AND THE SUBSEQUENT EXPANSION

At the end of hostilities, the *Uskmouth* resumed the peace-time pattern of trade. Guy started taking over the transactions in relation to the purchasing and sale of coal and spent an increasing part of his time on the Cardiff Exchange. The period following the First World War was one of great prosperity to shipowners as markets neglected in the war were restocked by industry returning to peace-time production. In consequence, ships were much in demand and were changing hands at up to ten times their pre war value. However this boom did not last and by the Summer of 1920 the crash came, taking with it a large number of South Wales shipowners who had invested all at the height of the trading cycle. Fortunately Richard W. Jones and Company had not been affected to any great extent, probably due to Bonn's natural reluctance to expand.

Meanwhile trade through Newport Docks had increased as follows:—

Year	Total Tonnage Handled	Coal & Coke Exports (tons)	Iron Ore Imports (tons)
1900	4,163,483	3,651,997	191,428
1910	5,787,983	4,976,484	168,675
1920	5,102,319	4,388,646	276,704

There were fluctuations however, and in 1921 iron ore imports accounted for only 27,275 tons.

Close connections had always been maintained with the Spanish and Italian coal importers, and the purchase of coal on behalf of these was maintained, but it became apparent that the once regular iron ore shipments to the United Kingdom were not going to sustain more than one ship. Guy and Alan desired to expand their shipping interests, and in an endeavour to achieve this sought to find a homeward cargo which would provide sufficient volume to warrant the acquisition of additional vessels. As a result, having discharged her coal cargo in Spain or Italy instead of sending the *Uskmouth* to Huelva to load the customary cargo of iron ore, she was sent to North Africa to load esparto grass. This product is used in the manufacture of high quality paper and was carried to the Firth of Forth for use in the Scottish Paper Mills. It is in connection with this trade that Richard W. Jones and Company became best known, requiring as it did, knowledge of the vagaries of the different ports and shippers and special skills in stowage.

It was to meet the requirements of this trade that the two brothers, who were more and more taking the decisions in relation to the business, decided to acquire a second ship. Bearing in mind that freight rates had slumped and that there was an abundance of good tonnage going cheap, they decided to purchase a ship from other owners instead of ordering a new vessel. As a result, in 1921 they acquired a four year old steamer of the three-island type which had been built in 1917 by Craig, Taylor and Co. Ltd., Stockton, as the *Firtree* for the Tree Steamship Co. Ltd. of Cardiff, and had passed two years later to the Maindy Shipping Co. Ltd., also of Cardiff as the *Maindy Forest*. This ship of 2,488 gross tons was the first of the three island type to join the fleet, the first acquired from other owners and was also the first built outside Sunderland. She was registered in the ownership of the Ukside Steamship Co. Ltd., renamed *Uskside* (2) and had been acquired at a fraction of the price that her namesake was sold for three years earlier.

So successful was this entry into the esparto trade, that in 1923 two new ships were ordered from the Burntisland Shipbuilding Co. Ltd. of Burntisland, Fife, being laid down as yard numbers 120 and 121. The first was delivered in that year as the *Uskhaven* and was joined the following year by the *Uskbridge*. Both were of the three island type and of 2,460 gross tons, and their delivery was to mark a long association between Richard W. Jones and Company and their builders. The building of these ships on the Firth of Forth was a clear reflection of the partners' new trading interests, with esparto grass to Scotland. The Chairman of the Burntisland yard, Sir Amos Ayre, his brother Wilfrid and their families became good friends of the Jones brothers.

The esparto was carried from North African ports such as Sfax and Sousse in Tunisia and others in Algeria, to the Firth of Forth, the outward cargoes of coal, having been purchased or fixed on the Cardiff Exchange were loaded in South Wales, but increasingly were being lifted from North East Coast ports. A feature of the ships' paying off in Scotland at Granton, Grangemouth or Methil, was the inclusion of an increasing number of Scots in the crew lists.

Alan Treverton Jones was married to Mildred, the daughter of Sir Abraham Garrod Thomas, the co-founder of the South Wales Argus, Chairman of the Royal Gwent Hospital at Newport, and a former Liberal Member of Parliament, and they had two children. However, tragically he died in 1924 at the age of 47, just when the expansion of the business was taking place. This was a major blow, as although Bonn was still a partner, Alan and Guy had taken over the reins and had been making plans for even further expansion.

Guy had married Joyce Rainforth of a well-known Newport family who had been in business as jewellers at the Westgate Square. In these circumstances Guy's brother-in-law Geoffrey Ford Rainforth, a chartered accountant, joined the partnership to ensure continuity. He, like Alan before him, and Guy, was to make a constructive contribution to the running of the business and its future expansion.

The Uskside Steamship Co. Ltd. comprised a fine fleet of modern ships as follows:—

Name	Year Built	Gross Tons
Uskmouth	1916	2,320
Uskside (2)	1917	2,488
Uskhaven	1923	2,464
Uskbridge	1924	2,466

Having achieved this great degree of expansion, and outlayed much of their capital resources, it was thought that there were still opportunities for further developments. In these circumstances in 1925 a family friend, Philip d'Ambrumenil (later to become Sir Philip and chairman of Lloyds who was married to Merriel, daughter of C. H. Bailey the founder of the well-known ship repairing company bearing his name which still has connections in South Wales) formed a company under the title of The Uskport Steamship Co. Ltd. and took delivery of the steamship *Uskport* from the Burntisland Shipbuilding Co. Ltd. She was in every respect a sister ship of the *Uskhaven* and *Uskbridge*. Richard W. Jones and Company were appointed managers of this company and its single ship, but after a short time acquired the full share capital in this company. The fleet was increased by these various transactions to five ships.

Geoffrey's role was to act as husband to the ships and manager of their day to day affairs, and to smooth the paths ahead of them by appointing and supervising port agents. Either directly or through the superintendents or masters he was responsible for crew matters, storing, victualling, bunkering, repair and maintenance of the ships, for arranging insurance at Lloyd's and through the P & I Clubs, and for finance. Guy continued to represent the partnership on the Cardiff Exchange, where he spent more than half his time buying coal and some pitwood and negotiating charters for the ships. Even in those days, before the decline in the importance of the Cardiff Exchange, the firm was using the Baltic Exchange in London and some of the foreign exchanges and it was Guy's job to appoint brokers to cover these markets and to fix the ships through them. The connections in Spain and Italy were very important to the business and the families of these major customers became firm friends of the Jones family. They were to have an association with one of these, the Giachetti family of Naples, for many years. The partners also expanded its interests to include agency work at Newport and shipbroking.

An indication of the smartness of the ships was reflected in their contract to carry coal to Monaco for the Monte Carlo Gas Company. Three cargoes a year were carried, a condition of the charter party being that the ships should be clean and in good order and the crew properly and smartly dressed particularly when ashore in this centre for tourism, where appearances were regarded as all important. The ships always had white upperworks, deck houses, masts and a bright yellow funnel, and it was their reputation in this connection that had ensured that they were awarded this contract. The Masters and officers looked forward to these calls at Monaco, as they were allowed free admission to the Casino. The partners made great efforts to share these voyages evenly amongst the ships to give all their personnel an opportunity to enjoy the facilities. The coal took ten days to unload at this port and, as the Masters were allowed to take their wives on one voyage per year, this was the one most favoured.

Although the main trading interests of Richard W. Jones and Company were in the Mediterranean, occasionally a charter was accepted in the Summer for a voyage to the Baltic or North Russia with coal outwards and timber or pit props homewards. The Miners' strike of 1926 and subsequent General Strike involved the ships in outward passages in ballast to the Mediterranean, but did not affect the plans for further expansion.

During 1927, Bonn retired from the partnership of Richard W. Jones and Company, leaving the business in the capable hands of his son and Geoffrey Rainforth. Two years later he died. At about this time the firm moved its offices from 112 Dock Street to much larger premises at 104.

In 1927 the *Uskmouth* was sold to other South Wales owners and after a number of changes of ownership she became a casualty of the Second World War when she sank off Hurd Bank, Malta on September 6, 1943. It was presumed that she had struck a mine. With the disposal of the *Uskmouth,* an order was placed for a replacement with the Burntisland yard, which appeared in 1928 in the form of a second *Uskmouth.*

The fleet was increased to six ships by the delivery the following year of the *Uskvalley* from Burntisland. The expansion was now complete and the partnership was a major Newport family shipowning enterprise.

In 1929 the fleet had achieved its greatest size. Although coal shipments from Newport Docks were maintained at something in excess of six million tons annually, iron ore imports had, by the following year, been suspended. The fleet at this time comprised the following steamers:—

Name	Year Built	Gross Tons
Uskside (2)	1917	2,488
Uskhaven	1923	2,464
Uskbridge	1924	2,466
Uskport	1925	2,462
Uskmouth (2)	1928	2,478
Uskvalley	1929	2,480

All the vessels were owned by the Uskside Steamship Co. Ltd. with the exception of the *Uskport* which was registered in the ownership of the Uskport Steamship Co. Ltd. The five ships built in the 1920s were of the same design and indeed were sisterships. The "Usk" ships were a truly fine fleet.

12. THE DEPRESSION

Unfortunately, hardly had this expansion of the fleet been completed than the depression of the early 1930s arrived. The business was by now in no way dependant on the trade through Newport Docks, although the figures relating to shipments show the gravity of the situation. Coal exports fell from 5 million tons in 1930 to a little over 2½ million in 1933, whilst in 1930, iron ore imports amounted to less than a thousand tons; there was none handled at the port during the following three years. In many respects, other ports fared even worse. Freight rates fell alarmingly as the amount of cargo available for shipment fell and matters were not helped by the same number of ships chasing what cargo there was.

In view of these poor trading conditions, although maintaining the requirements of the esparto trade, the ships found to be surplus for this requirement were diverted to other areas within the intermediate tramp trades. As a result, charters were undertaken to North Russia and the Baltic and while previously timber had never been a major cargo to them, they now loaded prepared timber and pit props for the United Kingdom. The general policy of laying up their ships as others had done during this period was resisted saying much for Guy's ability in securing charters. However it was felt that a fleet of six ships was now too large and as a result, two of them, the oldest, were disposed of. The *Uskside* (2) was sold during 1931 to Swedish flag operators and continued to trade until converted into a hulk in 1968. The *Uskhaven* was laid up for a few months in 1932 at Grangemouth and was subsequently sold to Constant's of Cardiff who resold her the following year to German owners as the *Marion Traber,* sailing as such until October 14, 1939, when she was wrecked near Oxelosund while on passage to Hamburg.

There is no doubt that the depression of the early thirties hit the companies very hard; it is indeed probably true that all the reserves that had been accumulated over the years had to be deployed and that even then the companies came very near to bankruptcy, in spite of the stringent economies that were made. With a large part of the merchant fleet laid up in the estuaries around Britain there were virtually no buyers available for the four remaining ships and even if there were the price that might have been obtained would have been insufficient to cover repayment of the outstanding mortgages. Further, the partners were very conscious of their obligations to keep as many as possible of their loyal crews in employment. The various other activities of the partners, including ship agency, broking and trading in coal were maintained as best they could. It is interesting to note that for some years, Richard W. Jones and Company had been responsible for the purchase and arranging the shipment from the North of England, of the salt used in the Winter months on the roads in Monmouthshire. They undertook this business on behalf of all the local authorities in the county and for the Monmouthshire County Council until well after the Second World War.

During 1932, the eldest of Guy's three sons, Dennis Ford Treverton Jones, who was aged 18, joined the business. Under the directions of his father and uncle he received training in all aspects of ship management, agency and brokerage, as well as the activities, now somewhat reduced, as merchants. It was decided to groom Dennis for the business as he had shown a great interest and much promise. In furthering his training, he was also sent abroad to get first hand experience and knowledge of shippers and to make connections. He spent a fruitful period with the firm's Bilbao agents. He was a linguist, having mastered Spanish and French, and this was felt to be a great asset.

Unfortunatelly on October 24, 1935, the six year old, most modern unit of the fleet, the *Uskvalley,* was lost when, with a Russian Pilot on board, she went ashore on Lyamitski Shoal, near Onega, on passage from Soroka to Cardiff or Barry with a cargo of timber. It was rumoured that the Russian Authorities shot the pilot as punishment for this incident. However on December 11 the ship was refloated by the Soviet Authorities and following repairs was placed in their Merchant fleet as the *Archangelsk,* trading as such until September 30, 1943 when she was torpedoed and sunk by the German submarine *U960* in the North Sea.

Eventually the depression started to lift and there was an improvement in the prospects. This was given impetus by the British Government introducing the "Scrap and Build" Scheme which granted low interest loans to British shipowners to build ships in British yards on the basis of one ton built for every two tons broken up. This enabled shipowners to modernise their fleets, reduced the number of ships engaged in world trades and provided much needed work at shipyards in the United Kingdom.

This move was an excellent opportunity for Richard W. Jones and Company to add a new vessel to the fleet of the Uskside Steamship Co. Ltd., and to take advantage of the scheme had to acquire a ship of roughly twice the size of the vessel they wished to build. Thus in 1936 they purchased a steamer of 5,240 gross tons, the *Ena G* for £10,500 from the Glenfield Syndicate Ltd. of London. This ship dated from 1918 and had been built to the order of the Shipping Controller as the *War Parrot,* and had passed shortly after to the Bank Line as their *Yoseric*. She had been owned by the Glenfield Syndicate for a matter of months only and when they sold her to the Uskside Steamship Co. Ltd. they made a loss as they had paid £14,250 for her. The ship was never traded by Richard W. Jones and Company, and they quickly resold her for breaking up to John Cashmore of Newport for the sum of £7,500. The £3,000 shortfall being well worth while in order to obtain the advantageous facilities offered by the British Government.

At this time, the oldest unit of the fleet the *Uskbridge* of 1924, was disposed of for further trading to Chilean buyers for whom she became the *Don Thompson,* surviving until 1959 when delivered to shipbreakers at San Antonio. Before work commenced on dismantling her, she was driven aground on July 25 during a gale and became a total loss.

After buying and selling the *Ena G* and disposing of the *Uskbridge,* an order was placed with Burntisland Shipbuilding Co. Ltd. for the construction of the new ship. The cost of the vessel was negotiated at a price of £47,953 and was laid down as yard number 204. The British Government allowed a £45,000 loan for the vessel over 12 years at 3% interest, with repayments deferred for two years. The new ship was launched by Sara the wife of Geoffrey Ford Rainforth on November 26, 1936, and was named *Uskside;* she was the third ship in the history of the fleet to be so named and was completed early the following year. She was also the first "Usk" ship to have a cruiser stern and at 2,706 gross tons was the largest vessel to be traded by the partners.

The Richard W. Jones and Company fleet now comprised three ships, the *Uskport* of 1925, *Uskmouth* (2) of 1928 and the *Uskside* (3) of 1937, and they were well placed to take full advantage of improvements in the intermediate tramp trades, no matter how small. During the Spanish Civil War, although high freight rates were offered for shipowners prepared to run the blockade, the partners decided not to send their ships into Spanish ports as they felt that their connections built up over many years would have been prejudiced for the future. However, many other owners, particularly in South Wales, decided to take advantage of the high rates and more than a few fortunes were made. One consequence of this was to see an improvement generally in freight rates.

Early in 1939, a virtual sistership of the new *Uskside* was ordered from Burntisland at a contract price of £66,861, clearly reflecting the inflationary times before the war. To build this ship, the partners were granted the facility of a loan of £60,000 under the Government Shipping Loan Scheme which had been introduced during that year. The shipbuilders took advantage of the Shipbuilding Grant to keep the price of the vessel as low and as competitive as possible.

13. THE SECOND WORLD WAR

Thus at the outbreak of the Second World War the fleet operated by Richard W. Jones and Company consisted of three ships, with another in the course of construction. Of these, one was to be sold in 1940, while the remaining three were lost as the result of enemy action. During the period of hostilities, the ships, whilst remaining under the management of the partners, were controlled as regards cargoes and directions by the Ministry of War Transport.

The first casualty was the *Uskmouth* (2) which was sunk by gunfire and torpedoes from the German submarine *U43* in the Bay of Biscay on November 25, 1939, during which action the Master, a long serving officer, Captain Smith and one other member of the crew were lost. At the time of her loss the ship had been on passage, unescorted, from Sunderland to Monaco with 3,900 tons of coal.

During 1940, with the imminent arrival of the new ship, it was decided to dispose of the *Uskport* in order to be able to pay outright for the new vessel without course to take up the Government's Shipping Loan of £60,000. The *Uskport* became the *Waldinge* for Constants of Cardiff, and on August 19 of that year was bombed and damaged by German aircraft while lying at Milford Haven. Having been repaired and returned to service, fifteen months later on November 19, 1941 she was torpedoed by a German E-boat in the North Sea and sank the following day.

With the sale of the *Uskport,* the new ship launched by Joyce the wife of Guy Treverton Jones arrived in the fleet in June, 1940 and was registered in the ownership of the Uskport Steamship Co. Ltd. She was named *Uskbridge* (2) and was of 2,615 gross tons. Hardly had she arrived than she became a war loss, when, on October 17 she was torpedoed and sunk by the submarine *U93* in the North Atlantic while on passage from Swansea to Montreal with a cargo of 4,000 tons of anthracite. Tragically two out of her crew of 29 were lost.

During 1940 two ships were placed under the management of the partners by the Ministry of War Transport, the *Empire Seaman* on April 19, 1940 and the *Empire Resistance* about four months later. The *Empire Seaman* (1,921 gross tons) had formerly been the German *Morea* and had been captured by H.M.S. *Hasty* West of Cape Finisterre on February 12 of that year, condemned as a prize and passed to Richard W. Jones and Company. However, the management ceased in December when she was scuttled as a blockship by the Royal Navy. The *Empire Resistance* (1,631 gross tons) had formerly been the Italian *Libano* captured by the Royal Navy in June, 1940, and having been condemned as a prize passed to the partners to manage.

A number of other ships were placed under the partners' management, including the Danish *Rolfsborg* which had diverted to a British port after the fall of Denmark and had been requisitioned by the Government. Additionally they took over the management of a number of neutral ships which had been time chartered by the Ministry of War Transport, as follows:—

Name	Gross tons
Bifrost	1,781
Hallbjorg	2,850
Hedrun	2,325
Norania	2,916
O. A. Brodin	1,960
Skoghaug	1,950

In July, 1941 the Ministry of War Transport placed the management of a new "Empire" ship, the *Empire Sedge* of 2,852 gross tons, in the hands of the partners. She was a collier and had just been completed by William Gray and Co. Ltd. at West Hartlepool. She, like all the ships managed on behalf of the Ministry, was allocated on the basis of the payment of a monthly management fee to the partners, no proportion of the vessel's earnings being involved. However this particular ship's management was transferred to others some three months later.

The last war loss suffered by the firm was their last owned ship, the *Uskside* (3). Under the command of Captain G. Fiddler she had taken part in the invasion and subsequent supply of Sicily and on August 1, 1943 was bombed and sunk by aircraft while at Palermo. Tragically, one member of the crew was lost. Following the war she was salved and by 1947 was trading as the Italian *Teseo,* in which guise Geoffrey Ford Rainforth was invited to lunch on board by the Italian Master when she was moored at Swansea in the early 1950s. The ship survived until December 24, 1955 when she was wrecked at Yamaniguey, near Baracoa, Cuba, while on passage Baracoa to Baltimore with a cargo of chrome ore.

During 1944 the management of another new "Empire" ship the *Empire Osborne* (2,922 gross tons) fresh from the yard of William Gray and Co. Ltd., West Hartlepool, was placed in the hands of the partners. She was of the three island design known as the Scandinavian type tramp ship. However, on December 20 of that year, under the command of Captain Fiddler she was mined in the River Seine. Although badly damaged, she was subsequently repaired and returned to service.

During the war, a number of loyal men had died while serving aboard the firm's ships as the result of enemy action. The following were decorated in recognition of their efforts:—

Captain Evans — M.B.E.
Captain Fiddler — O.B.E.
Boatswain Husband — B.E.M.
Chief Engineer Reeves — M.B.E.

Just after the end of hostilities, on July 13, 1945 the Danish *Rolfsborg* was lost while lying at anchor in Largo Bay, in the Firth of Forth, when another ship collided with her.

14. THE POST WAR RECOVERY

At the conclusion of hostilities Richard W. Jones and Company being without any of their own ships set about the task of rebuilding the fleet. The *Empire Osborne* was purchased from the Ministry of War Transport in 1946 under the British Government's Ship Disposal Scheme, renamed *Uskport* (2) and registered in the ownership of the Uskport Steamship Co. Ltd. Shortly after, a further ship joined the fleet, when the Uskside Steamship Co. Ltd. took over the contract for the steamer *Empire Warner* which was in course of construction by the Ailsa Shipbuilding Co. Ltd. at Troon to the order of the Ministry. This ship was completed as the *Uskside* (2,961 gross tons) in June, was the fourth ship to bear the name for the firm and was a sistership of the *Uskport*. By this time all the managed tonnage had been returned to their respective owners or direct to the Government.

At about this time the partners became managers of the Latvian steamer *Spidola* of 2,833 gross tons, built in 1905. The owner of this ship, P. Dannebergs, was domiciled in the United Kingdom after the disappearance of Latvia into the U.S.S.R. Her crew being displaced persons, treated the ship as their home, some having their wives permanently aboard; the ship was maintained to quite exceptionally high standards. The partners managed this ship until about 1952.

Dennis, who had left to serve with the Armed Forces during the war, returned to the business and was immediately made a partner. Unfortunately the war had delayed this recognition of his contribution to the firm, but he quickly started to take over the reins of the business in the next few years and both his father and uncle had great expectations of him.

The pattern of peace-time trade was resumed. The two war built ships were employed in the esparto trade homewards and in view of the rapid reduction of coal shipments from South Wales, took coal outwards from the North East ports. On occasions the vessels were sent in ballast to Archangel to load pitwood for the private collieries, later the National Coal Board, and for the first time, excluding war-time Government controlled sailings, they were sent across the North Atlantic to load timber on the Canadian East Coast for European ports. The partners continued as merchants, buying coal on behalf of clients in Spain and Italy and still arranging the purchase of road salt on behalf of local authorities in Monmouthshire. It is interesting to note that at the entry of Italy into the Second World War on the side of Germany, there were still sums of money outstanding to the partners in respect of coal shipments. Having always maintained good relations with the Italian coal importers, it was gratifying when these sums were settled after the war. Shipbroking and agency work continued as before the war.

Although the ships were rarely visiting the Bristol Channel with cargo, they were occasionally ballasted back to Barry or Cardiff for dry docking and surveys.

Tragically during 1950 Dennis died in hospital after a routine operation. This was a major blow as both his father and uncle were quite senior and Dennis was the natural successor to ensure the continuity of the business. As a result, two years later, Guy's other sons Paul and Brian joined the partnership. Paul Treverton Jones was a chartered accountant like his uncle while Brian Ford Treverton Jones had served in the Diplomatic Service of the Foreign Office. At this stage I should explain the earlier family connection with the South Wales Argus. This was an interesting one as Thomas, as earlier stated, was a co-founder and was its second chairman. Bonn also was among the founders but both families disposed of their shareholdings in the newspaper business in 1908. However Guy was enlisted as a local director in 1935 as was his son Paul in 1954, and both became chairmen, the latter still holding that office.

Meanwhile in 1951 there had been sufficient recovery to warrant the acquisition of a third ship and so another war built "Empire" ship was bought. Built in 1943 by William Gray and Co. Ltd., West Hartlepool, as the *Empire Valour,* she had passed to the Eskgarth Shipping Co. Ltd. in 1948 as the *Eskgarth,* and placed by the partners under the ownership of the Uskside Steamship Co. Ltd., she became the *Uskmouth* (3). In 1952 the Uskport Steamship Co. Ltd. was wound up, and in the same year another company bearing the same title was incorporated. The purpose of this operation was to release Dennis' share in the capital of the companies.

At this time the three ships were ,at the instigation of the two new partners, converted from coal to oil fired boilers. The work was carried out at Brigham and Cowan's yard at South Shields under the supervision of Graham Bullen of T. A. Reed Ltd. the partners' marine superintendents. Oil firing is cleaner, more economical to operate, more reliable, and required fewer engine room ratings, but the over riding benefit was its effect on the cargo capacity. On a normal round voyage to the Mediterranean the ship would leave the United Kingdom with maybe seven hundred tons of coal bunkers, but she would need less than half this amount of fuel oil since she could put in to Gibraltar or Ceuta to top up; the deadweight saved could be used for cargo.

For the following account of the trades that Richard W. Jones and Company were involved in, I am grateful to Mr. Paul Treverton Jones It gives a valuable insight into the complexities and difficulties experienced by the principals in a small family shipowning business at this time.

> I joined the firm in 1952 without much idea of what I was in for, although I had been employed by them for some years in a non-executive capacity. This was in the aftermath of the Korean War

which had caused a world wide shortage of tonnage. The first thing I learnt was that the freight market had collapsed almost overnight; the results of the voyages recently completed were extraordinarily good, the estimates for the voyages about to be undertaken showed that they could not possibly yield any profit at all. This caused my brother and I some consternation but I found that my two senior partners were quite unconcerned, so completely hardened were they to the fluctuations of the market. Applying hindsight it is obvious that there were few real grounds for optimism at that time and that the decline in the United Kingdom Shipping Industry was already under way. The joint evils—if they can be so described—of Flag Discrimination, heavily subsidised fleets and Flags of Convenience were to ensure that there would almost always be a surplus of ships to cargoes and the growth of the practise of time and bareboat chartering was to erode the share of the market which traditionally belonged to the true tramp owner. We did all the same have a few good years and were able to keep going by judicious disposal of the older ships when the times were right.

We thought then that the best policy would be to concentrate on the carriage of esparto grass in which we had some expertise and an entree to the best of the available orders through the coincidence that our London brokers, Chas Gee and Company, were also the main charterers' brokers. As a general rule we carried coal outwards from the East Coast of the United Kingdom or from the near Continental ports such as Rotterdam and Antwerp to West Italy or occasionally South Spain, and then ballasted across to North Africa. Esparto is a tough grass which is harvested in the hinterland of Libya, Tunisia and Algeria, and is used for the making of high quality paper and banknotes. Cargoes were invariably destined for the Scottish papermakers and were discharged at Granton on the Firth of Forth or at Methil, the latter being for the mills of our good friends Tullis Russel.

Apart from the basic freights, which being always negotiated on the open market, were largely at the mercy of economic factors over which we had little control, the profitability of voyages depended on two main factors: time occupied and tonnage lifted. A round voyage discharging in Italy and loading in North Africa could last anything from six to eight weeks, the deciding factor being usually the time spent in port. For example a full cargo of coal of say 4,000 tons could be loaded at Immingham in one day but would take four or five times as long to load across the estuary at Hull. The same cargo could be discharged at Savona in a day, but might take five days at Genoa. As the freight rate would probably be the same, a round voyage starting Immingham / Savona would show far better results than one starting Hull / Genoa.

Esparto is a very light cargo which is stowed in the holds and to a considerable height on deck. Ships do not load anywhere near down to their full deadweight, the limiting factor being the amount of cargo which can be carried on deck without impairing the stability and safety of the ship. Stowage calls for considerable skill from the Master and Mate, but is even more dependant on the condition of the cargo itself. Bales which have been mechanically compressed are small and heavy and provide the maximum payload, whereas bales which have been put together by camel-power are light and bulky and ships are not paid to carry air. A shipowner chartered to load at Tripoli in Libya, where both methods are used, would not know (unless the name of the shipper had been winkled out during the negotiations) whether he would be able to stow a maximum cargo of say 2,600 tons or a minimum of say 2,000 tons. Paradoxically, the smaller cargoes also took longer to ship and discharge because of the bulk of the bales. The loading ports in Algeria were Aezew, which was sought after because of the quality of the bales and the efficiency of the stevedoring, and Nemours which was much inferior. The Tunisian ports of Sfax and Sousse were at this time very rarely used. Although esparto is reputedly a combustable cargo there were no recorded cases of any "Usk" ship or cargo catching fire.

During the Summer season one or more ships would be detached from the Mediterranean trades. Although the intermediate tramp class of ship traditionally carries timber, the "Usk" ships did this only rarely. They concentrated on pitprops (until the collieries changed to using steel props) and pulpwood, which was imported to the United Kingdom and Continental ports for the manufacture of paper. Sometimes they would ballast out to Archangel, but more often they would go transatlantic to the maritime provinces of Canada—Nova Scotia and New Brunswick and many of the small ports in the St. Lawrence estuary. Here the Welsh were very welcome to the local people with their Breton ancestry; the Welsh speakers among the crews found that they were able to converse in what was almost a common language. Outward cargoes were rare and the norm was to ballast, but occasionally cargoes of china clay could be picked up in Fowey for discharge in Portland or Philadelphia.

The shipbroking side of the business prospered during this period, so much so that the interests of Clifford C. Jones Ltd. were acquired. During the Suez Crisis of 1956 the *Uskside* was requisitioned by the British Government to carry materials to the Middle East. The other two ships, *Uskport* and *Uskmouth,* due to the resulting upturn in the freight market thus caused, provided some good returns by their employment.

Taking advantage of an upturn in ship sales prices brought about by a temporary increase in freight rates, during 1957 the partners decided to dispose of the *Uskport*. She was sold to Cuban interests for whom she traded as the *Rio Damuji* until 1970 when she was wrecked near Punta Maya Light.

In 1957, Guy Treverton Jones died at the age of 75, having spent well over fifty years in the partnership. It can be said safely that the prosperity of the venture was due to his directions particularly during the 1920s when the partners first entered the esparto trade, through the difficult days of the depression of the early 1930s, and to the recovery following the Second World War.

15. A NEW SHIP IS ORDERED

Since the Second World War, there had been much discussion between the partners as to the advisability of ordering new tonnage, but, having operated the three war built steamships for many years, it was realised that plans would have to be made for their eventual replacement. The *Uskport,* as previously described, was sold at a temporary upturn in the freight market and was a deliberate decision to enable the partners to obtain the maximum capital towards the construction of a new vessel. The decision to build a new ship had been taken by the four partners prior to the death of Guy and the three survivors carried on with the plan.

Having built all their ships in British yards, the partners saw no reason to change this policy and as a result invited a number of shipbuilders to quote, including the Burntisland Shipbuilding Co. Ltd. (their traditional builders) and the Ailsa Shipbuilding Co. Ltd. of Troon. However, on the basis of an earlier delivery and the question of price, the order went to the latter company.

Richard W. Jones and Company had always operated steamships and did not feel that there was any reason to change from this policy. The advent of the motorship in the pre- and immediate post-war periods had largely gone unheralded in South Wales where traditions die hard, and as a result, the order was for a steamer. Mr. Bullen of the marine superintendents, T. A. Reed Ltd. was involved at all stages of the negotiations and with working out the specification with the builders.

A series of meetings were held between representatives of the shipbuilders and the partners before and after the contract for the vessel was signed and will I am sure prove of interest.

12th February, 1957

PROPOSED NEW VESSEL
FOR MESSRS. R. W. JONES & CO.

Notes taken at Meeting held in Troon
on Thursday and Friday, 7th & 8th February, 1957

Present:	Mr. G. F. Rainforth Mr. P. Treverton Jones Mr. Bullen Captain Fiddler	Messrs. R. & W. Jones & Co.
	Mr. J. Ritchie Mr. T. Mackenzie	Ailsa Shipbuilding Co. Ltd.

Hull Items:

1. On Thursday, preliminary designs for a 4,650 ton total deadweight vessel capable of a speed of 10½ knots in service were presented. The alternatives being a vessel having machinery and majority of accommodation at midships, and a vessel having machinery at aft end, majority of accommodation in same position, and deck officers' and navigation bridge at midships.
2. Trim and stability conditions for each design were presented.
3. The ballast condition drafts for the aft end design were unacceptable, but it was agreed that, as this design had many other desirable features, it should be further investigated with a view to redisposing the ballast to give drafts of about 16ft aft and 10ft forward. To assist in this the double bottom in Nos. 1 and 2 holds to be raised and in Nos. 3 and 4 holds dropped. Entire deep tank at midships to be used for oil fuel and settling tanks provided P & S in way of the boilers. Total oil fuel to be about 400 tons. Reserve oil to be carried in No. 4 double bottom tank. Entire space below boilers to be used for oil fuel. This tank to be permanently filled. Aft peak tank bulkhead to be stepped to provide a total of 120 tons of feed water. Reserve feed water to be carried under the engine. A total of 30 tons of drinking water to be carried in two tanks at the aft end of the machinery space. A duct keel to be fitted under the holds to house ballast and oil piping.
4. On Friday, ballast drafts of 15.75ft aft and 9.00ft forward were indicated after the modification previously mentioned. These were acceptable.
5. After consideration of cost it was agreed that the beam be increased by 6in to give an increase of approximately 50 tons in the total deadweight carried. Later, after consideration of increase in accommodation and boilers, it was indicated that this increase could not be given.
6. The accommodation layout was discussed at length and numerous changes asked for. On the Friday, sketches of the modified accommodation were presented and these, subject to minor modification, were acceptable.
7. The preliminary midship section was examined and accepted in principle, but scantlings to be submitted after Lloyd's approval. Hatches to be reduced to 25ft width. Minimum width between bulwark and hatch stays to be 8ft. Durastic fillets to be fitted at tank top between frames. Ceiling not to be fitted and tank top to be increased 20/25% above Lloyd's scantlings for tank top on which grabs are used. Plating to be all welded. Reverse frames to be flush riveted to tank top.

8. The specification was examined and the following changes asked for:—

Dimensions:	Length overall to be increased as required up to a limit of 337ft. Beam moulded to be 47ft. and extreme beam 47ft. 6ins.
Speed:	To be $10\frac{1}{2}$ knots in loaded service and 11 knots on loaded trial.
Sternpost:	To be of back post type.
Rudder:	To be "barn" door type for design purposes but to be drawn out for semi-balanced and "barn" door type for perusal of Mr. Bullen. Bearing to be "Pallister" type.
Framing:	Stringers to be welded to bulkheads at each end.
Engine Room Skylight:	To have quick closing arrangements from outside engine room to M.O.T. requirements.
Hatch Covers:	Vents not to be fitted on hatch covers. Tops of vents to be mushroom type.
Bulwarks:	Design to be based on 5ft. bulwarks but Owners to give an early decision on whether this is sufficient height.
Upholstery:	Smoke room, Captain's and Chief Engineer's rooms to have Dunlopillo cushions covered with "repp". Owners' suite, and Officers rooms to have hair cushions covered with "repp". In all other rooms cushions to be of hair and Lyanide.
Chairs:	Captain's and Chief Engineer's and Owners' suites to have easy chairs. Crew's chairs to be of Pel type.
P.O.'s Lockers:	To be of wood.
Crew's Lockers:	To be of steel.
Berths:	To have chain and spring bottoms.
Galley:	Refuse chute to be fitted with running water. Potato peeler to be provided. Water boiler 10 gallons. 5 gallons in pantries.
Beds:	All Officers' beds to be 3ft. 6ins. wide. Captain's and Chief Engineer's beds to have wood ends to match their furniture.
Cold Chambers:	Capacities to be as follows:— Handling room—200 cubic feet. Vegetable room—150 cubic feet. Meat room—250 cubic feet.

Weelhouse:	Two flag lockers to be provided.
Windows:	Windows are not to be fitted at main deck level.
Hot Water:	A steam to hot water calorifier to be fitted in the midship accommodation.
Plumber Work:	All sinks to be of stainless steel. Sanitary and fresh water pressure pumps to be electric. Washing troughs not to be fitted in the washplaces but a single laundry to be provided for the officers and crew.
Masts & Derricks:	Masts to be self supporting as far as possible. Top-masts to be retractable to allow the vessel through the Manchester Canal. The foremast table to be higher than the radar. Two portable cargo clusters per hold to be provided. Each Officer's room and recreation room to be provided with a 15 amp. plug. Portable electric motor to be provided for boat recovery. Aldis lamp to be operated from mains and battery.
Stearing Gear:	To be by Hastie.
Windlass:	By Clarke Chapman, enclosed type.
Capstan:	By Clarke Chapman, enclosed type.
Cargo Winches:	By Clarke Chapman, 7ins x 10ins.
Hawsers:	Reel to be of angle section with top bar. Reels to be suitable for next size of wire to that provided for vessel.
Canvas Outfit:	Covers not required for windlass, winches or capstan.
Compasses:	Baby giro to be provided.
Timber Freeboard:	Sockets and bridles only to be provided by Ailsa. Remainder Owners' supply.

Steam smothering to be fitted to the holds.

Having signed the contract for the construction of the vessel a further meeting was held:—

18th June, 1957.

SHIP NO. 504

Notes taken during discussions at Troon on 5th June, 1957 between Owners' and Ailsa Shipbuilding Co. Representatives.

Present:	Mr. Rainforth Mr. Treverton Jones Mr. Bullen Captain Irvine	For Owners.
	Mr. Ritchie Mr. Smith Mr. Mackenzie	For Ailsa Shipbuilding Co.

HULL

1. In view of the saving in oil fuel consumption due to discussion on type of main engines and superheat, the total quantity of oil fuel to be reduced to 380 tons, i.e. 295 tons in three deep tanks of equal capacity at midships and 85 tons in two settling tanks at wings of boiler room. Boiler room double tank to be eliminated and open floors fitted. Midships deep tanks to be piped for oil fuel and alternatively water ballast. Deep tanks as at present to be reduced two frame spaces in length, i.e. now 10 feet long.

2. Drafts were indicated for the ballast conditions with the above changes and with the upper fore peak and No. 4 D.B. tanks filled. It was agreed that these were satisfactory and that they, along with drafts and G.M.S. for the other conditions, would be confirmed after detailed weight calculations had been made and the lines plan completed.

3. Bulkheads of settling tanks and oil fuel bunkers to be cleaded with 2ins. white pine.

4. Screen bulkhead in boiler room to be omitted and boilers to be turned to face aft. Fore and aft passage to be arranged on centreline between boilers and not at sides as at present. Existing settling tank width to be increased to give the capacity indicated in item 1 of these notes.

5. Poop house front to be square across ship and not rounded as at present.

6. Boiler diameters to be reduced by 12 inches. Care to be taken that MacGregor covers are suitable for the loading of timber and esparto grass deck cargoes.

7. One accommodation ladder to be arranged at the after end and one shore gangway with swivel platform at midship accommodation.

8. Accommodation to be re-arranged so that:—

   Owners' bedroom is labelled Steward's room.

   Sliding doors to be fitted between Master's and Owners' dayroom. Label Owners' dayroom as ante-room or dayroom.

   Apprentices' room on lower bridge to be made 2nd Officer's room.

   House on main deck trunk top at midships to house 3rd Officer, Apprentices' room and study, bond locker, drying room and Officers' washplace. Beds to be fore and aft. Entrances to this house to be at the aft end and side entrances, eliminated.

The fourth "Uskside" was laid down as the "Empire Warner" for the Ministry of War Transport, but completed for the Uskside Steamship Co. Ltd. in 1946. (A. Duncan.)

In the English Channel, the "Uskside" was on passage from the St. Lawrence to the Thames with a cargo of Pulp Wood.

The "Uskside" outward bound with a cargo of coal from the North East Coast to Italy.
(Skyfotos Ltd.)

The "Uskmouth" (3) was acquired in 1951. She is shown homeward bound with a cargo of esparto grass.

The third "Uskmouth" in ballast. (World Ship Photo Library.)

Launch of the "Uskbridge" (3) at Troon on February 24, 1959 by Mrs. Sara Rainforth.

The "Uskbridge" as built by the Ailsa Shipbuilding Co. Ltd., Troon.

(A. Duncan.)

"Uskbridge" (3). (World Ship Photo Library.)

Lengthening of the "Uskbridge" at Troon: Entering dry dock at 11 a.m. on May 1, 1962.

Lengthening of the "Uskbridge" at Troon: Winch and wires set up to pull bow half forward at 2.30 p.m. on May 10, 1962.

Lengthening of the "Uskbridge" at Troon: The pull completed at 4 p.m. on May 10, 1962 leaving a forty feet gap.

Lengthening of the "Uskbridge" at Troon: Now out of dry dock, on June 26, 1962. The ship sailed the following day.

The lengthened "Uskbridge" (3) in the English Channel. (Skyfotos Ltd.)

The third "Uskport" was acquired in 1962 from the Tate and Lyle Group.

(A. Duncan.)

The "Uskport" was the only motorship to enter the fleet. (Skyfotos Ltd.)

The Offices of Richard W. Jones and Company 1929-1968, at 104 Dock Street, Newport.

On boat deck 3rd and 4th Engineers' rooms to be increased so that beds are fore and aft.

On the poop deck the Boys' room to be removed and the Chief Steward's room arranged at the fore end.

On the main deck the forward Donkeyman's room to be arranged for two boys. Aft of this there are to be rooms for three Donkeymen and three Firemen.

All Crew rooms on main deck to be improved in size due to length increase in poop by squaring the front.

9. Plate guards to be fitted over steam pipes at hatch sides in lieu of rod protection.

10. Additional and alternative ring bolts and cleats to be fitted on house bulkheads to assist in securing deck cargoes.

11. Six ring bolts to be arranged one on poop house, bulwark and at aft end of house P & S so that No. 4 hatch winches can be used for mooring in event of breakdown of the capstan.

12. Shelves in paint store to be subdivided making compartments approx. 3 feet by 3 feet to prevent paint tins sliding about.

13. Draft marks to be arranged at midships for about 4 feet. All marks to be arabic numerals.

14. Windows to be fanlight type.

15. In Carpenter's stores an emery wheel to be supplied in lieu of a grindstone and trough.

16. Bayonet type lock back catches to be fitted to all cabin doors.

17. Deadbeat type yale locks to be fitted to all store rooms in lieu of padlocks.

18. Additional clocks to be fitted in the Master's, Chief Engineer's, Mate‘s, 2nd Engineer's rooms and galley.

19. Hawsers and reels to be fitted in forecastle space.

20. Steam smothering to be reconsidered in view of Ministry of Transport Regulations.

MACHINERY INSTALLATION

1. *Main Engines*. To be of Christiansen & Mayer Design, Size 9. Built by Ailsa. No engine-driven pumps to be fitted other than Lubricating Oil Pump. Piston Valves to be of Moss Phillips make. Universal Metallic Packing to be fitted to all rods and spindles.

2. *Main Boilers.* 2 Boilers, each 13′6″ dia. x 11′6″ long. W.P. 220 lbs. per sq. ins. Arranged with furnaces aft. Superheaters to be of "Melesco" manufacture, and difference in cost between ordinary smoke tube type and Desuperheater type to be ascertained. Forced draught fan to be arranged so that an additional engine can be fitted at a later date.
3. *Air Pump.* Independent and of G & J Weir's manufacture.
4. *Standby Lub. Pump.* Of G & J Weir's manufacture.
5. *Bilge Pump.* Similar to General Service Pump.
6. *Oily Water Separator.* "Turbulo" type of 20 tons capacity.
7. *Lub. Oil Purifier.* To be "Sharples" make and a spare bowl to be supplied.
8. *15 k.w. Diesel Generator.* Additional cost of making this machine fully automatic to be ascertained.

The order was placed during the Summer of 1957 at a contract price of £495,000 and the keel was laid on February 27, 1958. The ship was launched a year later on February 24, 1959 by Sara the wife of Geoffrey Ford Rainforth, and underwent trials on May 7 of that year.

The new ship was named *Uskbridge,* the third to be allocated that name, and was registered in the ownership of the Uskport Steamship Co. Ltd. Designed for a service speed of 10½ knots, she was fitted with a double compound Christiansen and Mayer engine built under licence at Troon. She was the last steamship to be built by Ailsa Shipbuilding and was the only one to be completed by them with that type of engine.

Her registered dimensions were:—

Length:	317 feet b.p., 337 feet o.a.
Breadth:	47.5 feet.
Depth:	23.4 feet.
Tonnages:	3,610.76 gross.
	1,792.11 net.
	2,838.11 underdeck.
	4,700 deadweight.
	6,769 displacement.

16. THE LAST TEN YEARS

The *Uskbridge* had been designed primarily for the carriage of esparto grass, with a good cubic capacity and the best possible layout for the shipping of high deck cargoes, with high bulwarks to facilitate this. It was thought, incorrectly, that speed was of secondary importance and it is clear in retrospect that the choice of propulsion was wrong. Ironically, her launch coincided with the beginning of a decline in the esparto trade and an intensification of competition and as a result she carried very little of this commodity throughout her life. Her arrival brought the fleet up to three ships.

By the late 1950s it was being realised by the partners that the future in their traditional employment had little to offer and that unless they could break new ground they would be obliged to follow the example of the many small Welsh shipowners who had abandoned the industry despairing of making a living from it. Their London brokers, Chas. Gee and Company, being aware of the problem, put Richard W. Jones and Company in touch, through the Baltic Exchange, with Gouldings Fertilisers of Dublin. Gouldings were expanding their manufacture of superphosphate and increasing rapidly their import of the basic raw material from Morocco. Because of their limitations in storage capacity and the seasonal nature of the business, they were looking for a flexible shipping capacity which Richard W. Jones and Company were able to provide by combining it with their traditional employment; taking outward cargoes or ballasting to meet requirements. From small beginnings the trade built up, until at certain peak times as many as three "Usk" ships were employed at the same time.

Cargoes were loaded in Casablanca and occasionally at Saffi in a matter of hours and discharged at Cork or Dublin. In Cork, every ton of cargo was discharged by hand into tubs, yet often more than 5,000 tons would be discharged and the ship turned around in two working days. In Dublin, with more sophisticated equipment available, the turnround would rarely occupy less than four or five days. Fortunately for the firm, at that time the main plant was in Cork.

July 18 1960 marked the entry into the partnership of two long serving employees; Melville Charles Bird and Frederick Harold Lawson. The former had been with the firm since 1936 and was in charge of the agency and cargo handling departments but sadly he died at a young age after a few years in the partnership. The latter was originally employed by the partners' Cardiff agents D. Glen Jones Ltd. and transferred in the war years. He was in charge of finance and office management until his retirement in 1966.

In 1961 a further financial reorganisation of the shipping companies took place whereby the Uskside Steamship Co. Ltd. bought out the whole share capital of the Uskport Steamship Co. Ltd. The latter thereafter continued trading normally but as a subsidiary of the former company.

During the early 1960s, the involvement with the phosphate trade from Casablanca to Eire had developed to such an extent that the *Uskbridge,* which it had been discovered was the ideal ship for this trade with her wide unencumbered holds, was returned to her builders for lengthening. The *Uskbridge* had in many respects proved to be uneconomical in service and her lengthening by 40 feet in 1962 made her a more suitable vessel.

She had arrived at Troon on April 27, entered dry dock soon after, where her hull was cut through forward of the bridge, and with the use of winches, wires and jacks, the forward section was pulled forward and a 40 feet section was built into the hull. The vessel left Troon on June 27 and re-entered service. Her gross tonnage had been increased to 4,098.

At this time the *Uskmouth* was disposed of to Panamanian interests and she was eventually broken up in Greece in 1971. Her place was taken in the fleet by the acquisition of a motorship, the *Sugar Importer* from the Tate and Lyle Group. This ship of 4,024 gross tons had been built in 1955 by Hall, Russell and Co. Ltd., Aberdeen, and was the result of experiments by Tate and Lyle in the early 1950s in the carriage of sugar in bulk as opposed to bags. She had her engine and accommodation fitted aft and, being a motorship, was a more economic vessel than the recent steamers in the fleet. Renamed *Uskport,* she was the third ship in the firm's history to carry the name and was placed in the ownership of the Uskport Steamship Co. Ltd., and had the distinction of being the only motorship ever to be owned by the firm. This purchase was financed with a mortgage of £250,000 from the Ship Mortgage and Finance Co. Ltd.

This ship was purchased primarily for the Irish phosphate trade, but was generally employed in the Summer carrying woodpulp from Clarke City, a port in the Province of Quebec at the mouth of the St. Lawrence, to Gravesend or Rochester for the newsprint mills of Messrs. Reed. Woodpulp is baled like esparto and in appearance resembles thick blotting paper or thin cardboard. The deck cargoes were difficult to secure against the bad weather frequently met with in the North Atlantic and often part or the whole of it would be missing by the time the ship arrived in the Thames. The bad weather also found some weaknesses in the bottom plates of the ship which proved expensive to make good. This, it was felt, was because the ship's construction was not strong enough to correspond with her speed of 12/13 knots.

In 1963 an office was opened in Cardiff when the shipbroking business of D. Glen Jones Ltd. was acquired, and shortly after, to strengthen their interests in Cardiff, the old established firm of Sir James German and Co. (Cardiff) Ltd. was also acquired. The following year Geoffrey

Ford Rainforth retired from the business, having completed almost forty years in the partnership during which time he had made a great contribution to the smooth running of the fleet.

During 1965 it was decided to dispose of the last war-built ship and concentrate on trading their two more modern vessels. Thus the *Uskside* passed to Greek owners, who renamed her *Gero Michalos*. She traded as such until May 12, 1968 when she was lost at Alsyob during a cyclone.

Co-operation between Richard W. Jones and Company and Gouldings was far closer than is usual between owner and charterer and the decision in 1967 of the latter to switch all their business to the Eire flag, Irish Shipping Ltd., came as a shock to the owners at a time when they were actively seeking additional tonnage to accommodate anticipated increases in the Dublin end of the trade. With the collapse of their forward plans, Paul and Brian took a hard look at the whole of the propsects in the shipping industry and saw nothing therein to give them any confidence in the future. They decided therefore to dispose of the *Uskport*, which passed through numerous owners until her arrival at Inverkeithing on January 21, 1980 for breaking up. With the sale of this ship the mortgage was repaid.

This left them with the *Uskbridge* alone. It was decided to trade this ship for a further year, during which she was sent far afield in search of new markets, and on her last voyage became the only "Usk" ship to trade outside the Northern Hemisphere. But nothing was found to give them any encouragement and the inevitable decision was taken in 1968 to sell the ship. She traded thereafter under various owners until 1978 when she was delivered to shipbreakers at Cartagena, Columbia.

Having outlasted most of the small Bristol Channel family shipowners, it was decided in 1968 to close the business, as, in a highly speculative and cyclical industry, the risks had become out of all proportion to the gains and a single family base too small to support the kind of developments that were needed.

The offices at 104 Dock Street, Newport were closed and in that same year the Uskport Steamship Co. Ltd., having been stripped of all its assets, was sold as a shell to the Graig Shipping Co. Ltd. (Idwal Williams and Co. Ltd.) of Cardiff. The company was quickly renamed by them as the Garth Shipping Co. Ltd. and thereafter used as one of their subsidiaries in the operation of bulk carriers.Sir James German and Co. (Cardiff) Ltd. was sold to Lambert Bros. Ltd.

While the partnership terminated in 1968 it took a further seven years to wind up all the affairs of the group due to the inherent complications of an international shipping operation of this nature. The liquidation of the Uskside Steamship Co. Ltd. was finally completed in 1975.

Thus this Newport based shipowning business, which had been owned and managed by three generations of the same family, came to an end.

AND THE "USK" SHIPS WERE NO MORE.

APPENDICES

17. APPENDIX ONE

Partners in Richard W. Jones and Company

Name	Period in the Partnership
Richard William Jones 1843-1890	1875—1890
Thomas Jones 1844-1903	1875—1903
John Henry "Bonn" Jones 1853-1929	1890—1927
Guy Treverton Jones 1881-1957	1903—1957
Alan Treverton Jones 1877-1924	1910—1924
Geoffrey Ford Rainforth 1890-1973	1924—1964
Dennis Ford Treverton Jones 1914-1950	1946—1950
Paul Treverton Jones b.1918	1952—1968
Brian Ford Treverton Jones b.1919	1952—1968
Melville Charles Bird	1960—1965
Frederick Harold Lawson	1960—1966

18. APPENDIX TWO
Fleet List

Name & Period in Fleet	Gross Tons	History
Camargo 1880-1893	948	1880 built by Wm. Pickersgill and Sons, Sunderland, as *Camargo* for Richard W. Jones and Company; 3.11.1893 lost off Sully Island after collision with steamer *Biscaye,* on passage coastwise to Newport.
Salerno 1882	1,354	1882 built by Osbourne, Graham and Company, Sunderland, as *Salerno* for Richard W. Jones and Company; 1882 to Scrutton, Sons and Company, London; 1886 to Salerno Steamship Co. Ltd. (Scrutton, Sons and Company), London; 1893 to J. Bacon Ltd., Liverpool; 1897 to A. Brostrom and Son, Gothenburg, renamed *Hogland;* 1901 to Angf-Aktieb Tirfing (A. Brostrom and Son), Gothenburg; 1903 to Angf-Aktie. Goteborg-Manchester (K. O. F. Dalman), Gothenburg; 1910 to Akties Norlands (A. Monsen), Tonsberg; renamed *Norlands;* 2.5.1918wrecked near Godrevy Lighthouse, 3 miles E.N.E. of St. Ives Head, on passage Swansea to Rouen with coal.
Alassio 1883-1910	1,261	1883 built by Strand Slipway Company, Sunderland, as *Alassio* for Richard W. Jones and Company; 1906 transferred to Alassio Steamship Co. Ltd.; 1910 to J. N. Sanne, Uddevalla, renamed *Hafsten;* 1917 to Aktieb J. N. Sanne, Uddevalla; 1928 to Rederiet "Haisien" (Oscar A. Pabotn), Elleholm; 1934 to Rederi A/B Galeon (Torsten Hillerstrom), Malmo, renamed *Galeon;* 1949 same owners, managers changed to Ture Hillerstrom; 8.1.1953 arrived at Gateshead for breaking up by J. J. King and Company.
Bergamo 1884-1897	1,208	1884 built by Wm. Pickersgill and Sons, Sunderland, as *Bergamo* for Richard W. Jones and Company; 1897 to Hans Kiaer and Company, Drammen, renamed *Prosum;* 1900 to Dampskibsacties Prosum (Hans Kiaer and Company), Drammen; 1903 to Acties Dampsk. Banheur (Fred Olsen), Drammen; 1905 owners restyled

Name & Period in Fleet	Gross Tons	History
		as Acties. Banheur, same managers; 24.10.1908 wrecked at Thornton-Lock, Innerwick, on passage London to Grangemouth in ballast.
Durango 1884	1,200 approx.	1884 built by Osbourne, Graham and Company, Sunderland, as *Durango* for Richard W. Jones and Company; 27.11.1884 lost S.W. of Dungeness after collision with barque *Luke Bruce,* on passage Dunkirk to Genoa.
Ricardo 1889-1891	1,246	1889 built by Wm. Pickersgill and Sons, Sunderland, as *Ricardo* for Richard W. Jones and Company; 10.4.1891 lost near Cape St. Mary after collision with *Adelphi Couppa,* on passage Huelva to the Mersey.
Elorrio 1894-1913	1,347	1894 built by Wm. Pickersgill and Sons, Sunderland, as *Elorrio* for Richard W. Jones and Company; 1906 transferred to Elorrio Steamship Co. Ltd.; 1913 to Blom's Rederiaktieb, Nookopng, renamed *Barbro;* 1917 same owners, managers changed to J. M. Dannberg; 1921 to Aug. Bolten. Wm. Miller's Nachfolger, Hamburg, renamed *Bolero;* 1925 to Rederi A/B Barbro (O. Edstrom), Stockholm, renamed *Barbro;* 1925 to Limhamns Rederi A/B (Edv. Persson), Limhamy, renamed *Edvard;* 1935 to L-u "Eeroo" (Karl Mitt), Tallinn, Estonia, renamed *Helios;* 1940 to I. Fagraeus, Stockholm, renamed *Selene;* 1946 port of registry changed to Jarna; 1953 to Companhia Naviera Minories S.A., Panama, renamed *Heros;* 12.2.1954 arrived at Dunstan for breaking up by Clayton and Davie.
Uskside (1) 1913-1918	2,066	1913 built by J. Priestman and Company, Sunderland, as *Uskside* for Uskside Steamship Co. Ltd.; 1918 to Pelton Steamship Co. Ltd., Newcastle, renamed *Largo;* 1946 to E. Hsiang Steamship Company (Chinese), renamed *Foo Nan;* 1951 to Kwang Hua Nav. Co. Ltd. (National China), renamed *Kwang Hua;* 1952 reported to have had engine trouble, made port and presumably broken up soon after.
Uskmouth (1) 1916-1927	2,320	1916 built by J. Priestman and Company, Sunderland, as *Uskmouth* for Uskside Steamship Co. Ltd.; 1927 to Ensign Shipping Co. Ltd. (Dunn and Company), Newport, renamed

Name & Period in Fleet	Gross Tons	History
		Ensign; 1933 to Constants (South Wales) Ltd., Cardiff, renamed *Wrotham;* 1935 to Calpean Shipping Co. Ltd., Gibraltar, renamed *Ensign;* 1935 to Chellew Steamship Management Co. Ltd. (F. C. Perman), London; 1937 back to Constants (South Wales) Ltd., port of registry now London, renamed *Sellinge;* 6.9.1943 sank off Hurd Bank, Malta, presumed to have struck a mine; c1947 salved and entered service for Achille Onorato, Naples as *Silvia Onorato;* 2.1.1948 wrecked on the East Goodwins, on passage Rijeka to Rotterdam with lead ore.
Uskside (2) 1921-1931	2,488	1917 built by Craig, Taylor and Co. Ltd., Stockton, as *Firtree* for the Tree Steamship Co. Ltd. (Howard Jones and King), Cardiff; 1919 to Maindy Shipping Co. Ltd. (Jenkins, Richards and Evans Ltd.), Cardiff, renamed *Maindy Forest;* 1921 to Uskside Steamship Co. Ltd., renamed *Uskside;* 1931 to Rederi A/B Bifrost (Jarl R. Trapp), Gothenburg, renamed *Agne;* 1943 same owners, managers changed to G. Karlberg; 1947 same owners, managers changed back to Jarl R. Trapp; 1951 to Rederi A/B Orvar (Yngve Fange), Helsinborg, renamed *Orvar;* 1952 to Rederi A/B Kullaberg (A. Sjosten), Hoganas, renamed *Hanna;* 1962 to Ilmari Tuuli, Finland, renamed *Teno;* 1967 to Antii Lempiainen O/Y Helsingfors, renamed *Eljes;* 1968 converted for use as a storage hulk in Norway.
Uskhaven 1923-1932	2,464	1923 built by Burntisland Shipbuilding Co. Ltd., Burntisland, as *Uskhaven* for Uskside Steamship Co. Ltd; 1932 to Constants (South Wales) Ltd., Cardiff; 1933 to W. Traber and Company, Hamburg, renamed *Marion Traber;* 14.10.1939 wrecked near Oxelosund, on passage to Hamburg.
Uskbridge (1) 1924-1936	2,466	1924 built by Burntisland Shipbuilding Co. Ltd., as *Uskbridge* for Uskside Steamship Co. Ltd.; 1936 to Cia. Carbonifera e Indistrial de Lota, Valparaiso, renamed *Don Thompson;* 1948 to Naviera Chilena del Pacifico S.A., Valparaiso, renamed *Algarrobo;* 1959 to shipbreakers at San Antonio, Chile, but was driven aground there on 25.7.1959 during a gale, and

Name & Period in Fleet	Gross Tons	History
		was so badly damaged that it was not considered worth salving her for demolition.
Uskport (1) 1925-1940	2,462	1925 built by Burntisland Shipbuilding Co. Ltd., Burntisland, as *Uskport* for Uskport Steamship Co. Ltd., 1940 to Constants (South Wales) Ltd., Cardiff, renamed *Waldinge*; 19.8.1940 bombed and damaged by German aircraft at Milford Haven; 19.11.1941 torpedoed by German E-boat in the North Sea off Aldeburgh in position 52.56N, 02.01E, and sank the following day.
Uskmouth (2) 1928-1939	2,478	1928 built by Burntisland Shipbuilding Co. Ltd., Burntisland, as *Uskmouth* for Uskside Steamship Co. Ltd.; 25.11.1939 sunk by torpedo and gunfire from *U43* in the North Atlantic in position 43.22N, 11.27W, on passage from Sunderland to Monaco with 3,900 tons of coal. 2 crew lost.
Uskvalley 1929-1935	2,480	1929 built by Burntisland Shipbuilding Co. Ltd., Burntisland, as *Uskvalley* for Uskside Steamship Co. Ltd.; 24.10.1935 ashore on Lyamitski Shoal, near Onega, on passage Soroka to Cardiff or Barry with timber, and abandoned; 11.12.1935 refloated by Soviet Authorities, and following repairs joined the Soviet fleet as *Archangelsk;* 30.9.1943 torpedoed and sunk by *U960* in the North Sea.
Ena G 1936	5,240	1918 built by Sir James Laing and Sons Ltd., Sunderland, as *War Parrot* for the Shipping Controller; 1920 to Andrew Weir and Co. Ltd., London (Bank Line); renamed *Yoseric;* 1936 to Glenfield Syndicate Ltd., London, renamed *Ena G;* 1936 to Uskside Steamship Co. Ltd. but not traded by them; 1936 broken up at Newport by J. Cashmore Ltd.
Uskside (3) 1937-1943	2,706	1937 built by Burntisland Shipbuilding Co. Ltd., Burntisland, as *Uskside* for Uskside Steamship Co. Ltd.; 1.8.1943 bombed and sunk by aircraft at Palermo; 1 crew member lost; c1946 raised, and by 1947 entered service for Societe Ligure di Armamento, Genoa, as *Teseo;* 24.12.1955 wrecked at Yamaniguey, near Baracoa, Cuba, on passage Baracoa to Baltimore.

Name & Period in Fleet	Gross Tons	History
Uskbridge (2) 1940	2,615	1940 built by Burntisland Shipbuilding Co. Ltd., Burntisland, as *Uskbridge* for Uskport Steamship Co. Ltd.; 17.10.1940 torpedoed and sunk by *U93* in the North Atlantic in position 60.40N, 15.50W, on passage Swansea to Montreal with 4,000 tons of anthracite. Of her crew of 29, 2 were lost.
Uskport (2) 1946-1957	2,922	1944 built by Wm. Gray and C.. Ltd., West Hartlepool, as *Empire Osborne* for Ministry of War Transport, managers—Richard W. Jones and Company; 20.12.1944 damaged by a mine in River Seine; 1946 to Uskport Steamship Co. Ltd., renamed *Uskport;* 1957 to Banco Cubano del Comercio Exterior, Cuba, renamed *Rio Damuji;* mid-1970 wrecked 3½ miles from Punta Maya Light, in position 23.06N, 81.25W.
Uskside (4) 1946-1965	2,961	1946 built by Ailsa Shipbuilding Co. Ltd., Troon; laid down as *Empire Warner* for Ministry of War Transport, but completed as *Uskside* for Uskside Steamship Co. Ltd.; 1965 to N. Michalos and Sons Maritime Co. Ltd., Greece, renamed *Gero Michalos;* 12.5.1968 lost at Alsyab during a cyclone. She had arrived there 27.4.1968 and was about to sail for Ceylon.
Uskmouth (3) 1951-1962	2,906	1943 built by Wm. Gray and Co. Ltd., West Hartlepool, as *Empire Valour* for Ministry of War Transport, managers—Glen and Co. Ltd.; 1948 managers changed to Eskgarth Shipping Co. Ltd.; 1948 to Eskgarth Shipping Co. Ltd., renamed *Eskgarth;* 1951 to Uskside Steamship Co. Ltd., renamed *Uskmouth;* 1962 to Cia. Merabello San Nicolas, Panama, renamed *Alexandra K;* 1968 to Pateras Bros. Ltd., Greece, renamed *Aristiois II;* 1969 to Reinato Marino Navegacion S.A., Panama; 1971 broken up in Greece.
Uskbridge (3) 1959-1968	3,611	1959 built by Ailsa Shipbuilding Co. Ltd., Troon, as *Uskbridge* for Uskport Steamship Co. Ltd.; 1962 lengthened 40 ft. by original builders, gross tonnage increased to 4,098; 1968 to Momba Shipping Corp., Liberia, renamed *Dynas;* 1974 to St. Nicholas Steamship Ltd., Bermuda, renamed *Transmar Venture;* 1976 to

Name & Period in Fleet	Gross Tons	History
		Renaissance Nav. Corp., Panama, renamed *Cape Verde;* 1977 to Cape Verde Nav. Inc., Panama; On or about 11.7.1978 arrived at Cartagena, Colombia for breaking up by 'Sipsa', 1.3.1979 demolition commenced.
Uskport (3) 1962-1967	4,024	1955 built by Hall, Russell and Co. Ltd., Aberdeen, as *Sugar Importer* for Silvertown Services Ltd., London; 1962 to Uskport Steamship Co. Ltd., renamed *Uskport;* 1967 to Cie. Maritime et Commerciale du Sud-quest, France, renamed *Laroche;* 1973 to Nigrita Cia. Nav. S.A., Greece, renamed *Macedonia;* 1976 to Macedonia Cia, Naviera, S.A., Greece; 1978 to Nigrita Cia. Nav. S.A., Greece; 1979 to Sunteam Maritime Co., S.A., Greece; 21.1.1980 arrived at Inverkeithing for breaking up by T. W. Ward Ltd.

19. APPENDIX THREE

Ships Managed on Behalf of the Ministry of War Transport

Name & Period Managed	Gross Tons	History
Empire Seaman 1940	1,921	1922 built by Schiffs -u. Dockbauw Flender A. G. Siems, Lubeck, as *Morea* for Hamburg-Amerika Linie) (Deutsche Levante Linie), Hamburg; 1935 to Deutsche Levante-Linie Hamburg A.G. (Deutsche Levante Linie G.m.b.H.), Hamburg; 12.2.1940 captured by H.M.S. *Hasty* West of Cape Finisterre in position 41.50N, 15.22W, condemned as a prize and allocated to Ministry of War Transport, 19.4.1940 managers—Richard W. Jones and Company; renamed *Empire Seaman;* 4.12.1940 scuttled as a blockship, location not known.
Empire Resistance 1940-1946	1,631	1908 built by Fevigs Jermskibsbyg, Fevig, as *Ottar* for A/S Ottar (J. C. Knudsen), Porsgrund; 1924 same owner, managers changed to Chr. Knudsen; 1935 to Servizio Italo-Portoghese Soc. Anon di Nav., Genoa renamed *Libano;* 6.1940 captured by Royal Navy, placed under Ministry of War Transport, managers—Richard W. Jones and Company, renamed *Empire Resistance;* 1946 to Resistance Shipping Co. Ltd., London, renamed *Resistance;* 1949 to Giacomo Costa fu Andrea, Genoa, renamed *Beatrice C;* 1954 to Raffaele Romano, Naples, renamed *Acilia;* 1956 to Apostolo and Ruffino S.R.L., Genoa, renamed *Cilin;* 1959 broken up at Savona.
Empire Sedge 1941	2,852	1941 built by Wm. Gray and Co. Ltd., West Hartlepool, as *Empire Sedge* for Ministry of War Transport, managers—Richard W. Jones and Company; 1941 managers changed to Wm. Cory and Son Ltd.; 1943 managers changed to Burnett Steamship Co. Ltd.; 16.10.1945 to Burnett Steamship Co. Ltd., renamed *Holmside;* 1956 to Shamrock Shipping Co. Ltd. (C. S. Brown), Larne, renamed *Gransha;* 1960 to Paolo Tomei, Italy, renamed *Daniela T;* 1963

Name & Period Managed	Gross Tons	History
		to "Capo Mannu" Soc. di Nav. S.p.A., Italy; 1972 to Mediterranea Marittima Sarda S.p.A., Italy, renamed *Vulca.*
Rolfsborg 1941-1945	1,825	1915 built by Fredrikstad Mek. Fredrikstad, as *Skard* for Alaskule (B. A. Sanne), Oslo; 1931 to A/S Furulund (Odd. Berg), Oslo, renamed *Kollskegg;* 1936 to J. A. Zachariassen and Company, Nystad, renamed *Rolsborg;* 12.1941 following the fall of Denmark placed under the Ministry of War Transport, managers—Richard W. Jones and Company, saw service as an Admiralty Collier; 13.7.1945 lost in collision at anchor in Largo Bay, Firth of Forth. Voyage Immingham to Aarhus with coal.
Empire Osborne 1944-1946	2,922	See *Uskport* (2) in Appendix Two for details.

In addition to the above vessels, the partners were also appointed to manage a number of ships which were time-chartered by the Ministry of War Transport, as follows:—

Name	Year Built	Tons Gross
Bifrost	1923	1,781
Hallbjorg	1919	2,850
Hedrun	1920	2,325
Norania	1907	2,916
O. A. Brodin	1920	1,960
Skoghaug	1930	1,950

20. APPENDIX FOUR

S.S. "CAMARGO"—Share Transactions 1880-1893

Date	No. of Shares	Transferred From	Transferred To
27. 7.1880	64	Registered at the Custom House, Newport,	Richard William Jones and Thomas Jones, jointly.
27. 7.1880	1	Richard William Jones and Thomas Jones, jointly.	Thomas Kemp, Master Mariner, 4 Eveswell Ter., Maindee, Newport.
27. 7.1880	2	,,	John Henry Robinson, Railway Contractor, Westminster Chambers, Westminster.
27. 7.1880	2	,,	Thomas Reynolds, Civil Engineer, 3 Clements Lane, London.
28. 7.1880	2	,,	George Louis Morton, Engineer, Farlton Crt., Harlesdon Road, Willesdon Middx.
30. 7.1880	2	,,	Henry Tothill, Analytical Chemist, 5 Park St., Newport.
30. 7.1880	1	,,	William Mullock, Stationer, Newport.
30. 7.1880	3	,,	Michael Thomas Brian, Coal Shipper, 1 Clytha Crescent, Newport.
31. 7.1880	1	,,	Rowland John Nicholas, Shipping Agent, 72 Stow Hill, Newport and James Henderson Winn, Shipping Agent, York Place, Newport, jointly.
31. 7.1880	2	,,	Edward Handfield Morton, Engineer, 12 Eaton Rd., Llaughton, Birkenhead, Chester.

Date	No. of Shares	Transferred From	Transferred To
6. 8.1880	4	,,	James Stratton, Farmer, Chilcombe, Winchester, Hampshire.
31. 8.1880	1	,,	William Denton, Ship Surveyor, Kymin Terr., Penarth, Glamorgan.
6. 1.1881	1	,,	Alfred Wilkinson Jones, Mechanical Engineer, Dash Wood House, London.
7. 1.1881	1	,,	Thomas Le Pelley, Master Mariner, Brock Cottage, St. Sampsons, Guernsey.
25. 1.1881	1	,,	John George Walton, Engineer, Tunstal Terr., Sunderland, Co. Durham.
10. 2.1881	2	,,	Susan Broadley, Widow, Barton Castle, Bath, Somerset.
3. 5.1881	1	,,	George Edward Gerge Andrews, Gentleman, Rimpton, Sherbourne, Dorset.
5. 5.1881	1	,,	Edwin Slade, Gentleman, Bedminster, Dorset.
8. 6.1881	1	,,	Walter Liberty Vernon, Architect, Clytha House, London Rd., St Leonards on Sea.
6.10.1881	1	,,	George Sparke, Colliery Agent, Newport.
18. 4.1882	1	Thomas Le Pelley	Richard William Jones and Thomas Jones, jointly.
21. 7.1882	1	Richard William Jones and Thomas Jones, jointly	Walter Runciman, Master Mariner, 12 Salmon St., South Shields, Co. Durham.
24. 7.1882	1		Charles Cullum, Secretary to a Public Company, Caerau Pk., Newport.

Date	No. of Shares	Transferred From	Transferred To
27. 7.1882	2	,,	Michael Brian, Coal Shipping Contractor, 26 Lime St., Newport.
9.12.1882	1	,,	John George Walton, Engineer, 10 Tunstall Terr., Sunderland, Co. Durham.
4. 3.1883	2	,,	Rochester Quinton, Architect, 2 Tudor St., City of London.
2. 4.1883	5	,,	William Davies, Gentleman, Bridgend House, Stonehouse, Gloucestershire.
12. 5.1883	1	,,	Emily Mary Connolly, Spinster, 68 Lee Rd., Blackheath, Kent.
4. 8.1883	1	Walter Liberty Vernon	Robert Vernon, Gentleman, Bower Hayes, High Wycombe, Buckinghamshire.
11. 9.1883	2	Richard William Jones and Thomas Jones, jointly.	Gertrude Wilhelmina Colborne, Spinster, The Vicarage, Leonard Stanley, Stonehouse, Gloucestershire.
5.11.1884	20	,,	MORTGAGE "A"—To secure sum due on account current and interest with Mary Elizabeth Jayne, Spinster, 4 Clytha Sq., Newport.
31.10.1884	1	Robert Vernon	Robert Vernon died on 31.10. 1884—Will with two Codicils dated respectively 20.5.1880, 14.3.1882 and 15.11.1883 appointing Robert Davenport Vernon and Edward Wilkins executors — Probate granted to them by the District Registry attached to the Probate Division of Her Majesty's

Date	No. of Shares	Transferred From	Transferred To
			High Court of Justice at Oxford on 5.12.1884. Share passed to Robert Davenport Vernon, Ironmonger, and Edward Wilkins, Solicitor, jointly, both of High Wycombe, Buckinghamshire.
10. 6.1885	1	Robert Davenport Vernon and Edward Wilkins, jointly.	Walter Liberty Vernon, Architect, Neutral Bay, Sidney, New South Wales, Australia.
12.10.1885	1	Walter Runciman	Richard William Jones
29. 3.1886	3	Michael Thomas Brian	James Theophilus Clements, Wagon Agent, Brooklea, Gold Tops, Newport.
30. 3.1886	3	James Theophilus Clements	MORTGAGE "B"—To secure sum of £125 at interest of 10% with John Young, Auctioneer, Tredegar Pl., Newport.
15. 4.1886	1	Thomas Kemp	Richard William Jones and Thomas Jones, jointly.
16. 7.1886	1	James Henderson Winn and Rowland John Nicholas, jointly.	James Henderson Winn, Merchant, Caerau Pk., Newport.
23. 8.1886	3	John Young.	MORTGAGE "B" Discharged by John Theophilus Clements.
23. 8.1886	3	John Theophilus Clements	Richard William Jones and Thomas Jones, jointly.
30. 8.1886	1	Richard William Jones and Thomas Jones, jointly.	Fred Vaughan, Solicitor, Newport.
6. 9.1887	1	Walter Liberty Vernon, Attorney, and Francis Griffin (With power of Attorney).	Richard William Jones and Thomas Jones, jointly.
2. 2.1888	1	Fred Vaughan	,,

Date	No. of Shares	Transferred From	Transferred To
31.12.1888	5	William Davies	William Davies died 31.12. 1888. Will dated 21.1.1884 and codicil thereto 29.7.1885 appointing Jane Charlotte Davies, Wm. Davies and Edward Palling Iittle as Executors. Probate granted in District of Gloucester 27.2.1889. As a result shares passed to Jane Charlotte Davies, Widow, Bridgend Ho., Stonehouse, Gloucester, Wm. Davies, Squire, Alberton Grange, Eastington, and Edward Palling Little, Solicitor, Stroud, jointly.
16. 7.1889	1	Jane Charlotte Davies, William Davies, and Edward Palling Little, jointly.	John George Walton, Engineer, 26 Fenchurch St., London.
16. 7.1889	4	,,	Richard William Jones and Thomas Jones, jointly.
23.11.1889	2	Edward Hadfield Morton	,,
18. 7.1890	20	Mary Elizabeth Jayne	MORTGAGE "A" Dischargeed by Richard William Jones and Thomas Jones, jointly.
21. 7.1890	31	Richard William Jones, and Thomas Jones, jointly.	Death of Richard William Jones, burial certificate dated 21.7.1890. Shares passed to Thomas Jones.
22. 7.1890	3	Thomas Jones	Bonn Henry Jones, Merchants Clerk, "Tregleath", Gold Tops, Newport.
10. 7.1890	1	Richard William Jones	Richard William Jones died 26.4.1890. Will dated 21.1. 1878 appointing Helen Jones as Executor. Probate granted

Date	No. of Shares	Transferred From	Transferred To
			in the District Registry, Llandaff 10.7.1890. Share passed to Helen Jones, Widow, "Caergwyn", Newport.
22. 7.1890	1	Helen Jones	Bonn Henry Jones
13.11.1890	1	George Sparke	George Sparke died 13.11. 1890. Will dated 15.10.1873 appointing Annie Bartlett Sparke as Executor. Share passed to Annie Bartlett Sparke, Widow, Olive Mount, Maindee, Newport.
12. 1.1891	1	Annie Bartlett Sparke	Thomas Jones
13. 4.1891	1	George Edward Genge Andrews	,,
4. 3.1892	2	Thomas Reynolds, Junior	,,
11.11.1892	2	George Louis Morton	,,
4. 3.1893	2	Henry Tothill	,,
18. 9.1893	1	William Mullock	Henry Oliver, Civil Engineer, Caerau Park Road, Newport.

On November 3, 1893, the vessel was lost in the Bristol Channel, and the Register at the Customs House, Newport was endorsed as follows:—

> Ship sunk off Sully on 3rd November, 1893 and in the opinion of the Managing Owner was a total loss as per his letter dated 7th November, 1893 in which he also states that the certificate is on board the vessel.
> Registry Closed 7th November, 1893.

21. APPENDIX FIVE

S.S. " USKBRIDGE "—Transcript of Ship's Register

The *Uskbridge* (3) was originally registered at Newport on May 4, 1959 being entry number 3 for 1959. However, following her lengthening this entry was closed and she was re-registered on June 15, 1962 as entry number 1 for 1962. The Transcript of the Ship's Register of the latter entry is reproduced on the front and back end papers. Note that the ship was later remeasured and that some entries are crossed out and the new particular is included.

Number of decks	One
Number of masts	Three Masts and One Derrick post.
Rigged	Not.
Stem	Clipper
Stern	Cruiser
Build	Clencher
Framework and description of vessel	Steel Cargo.
Number of bulkheads	Eight W.T.

	Feet	Tenths
Length from fore part of stem to the aft side of the head of the stem post ...	364	3
Main breadth to outside of plating ...	47	2
Depth in hold from tonnage deck to ceiling amidships ...	23	4
Depth in hold from upper deck to ceiling amidships, in the case of three decks and upwards ...	-	-
Depth from top of deck at side amidships to bottom of keel ...	26	6
Round of beam ...	0	9
Length of engine room, if any ...	60	0

PARTICULARS OF PROPELLING ENGINES, etc. (if any), as supplied by builders, owners, or engine makers

No. of sets of engines	Description of engines	Whether British or foreign made	When made	Name and address of makers	Reciprocating engines: No. and diameter of cylinders in each set	Reciprocating engines: Length of stroke	Rotary engines: No. of cylinders in each set	N.H.P. B.H.P. I.H.P. Estimated speed of ship
One	Reciprocating Steam Direct Acting.	Engines: British	Engines: 1959	Engines: Ailsa Shipbuilding Co. Ltd. Troon	Four	900	-	273·2. 1530
No. of shafts	Particulars of boilers - Cylindrical. Marine.	Boilers	Boilers	Boilers				